The Seeker

of

Well-Being

Retrieve balance in accordance with self

Indrajit GARAI

The rights to publish this book

For the French language: A part of this book was published under the title 'L'alchimie du bien-être' in May 2010 by Les Éditions du Dauphin, who has the rights for the traditional paper formats. All rights for electronic and audio books, as well as dramatic realizations, remain exclusive property of Indrajit GARAI

For all other languages: All rights remain exclusive property of Indrajit GARAI

Published by Indrajit GARAI, November 2015.

For the mother of my child

Table of contents

Prologue

Every writer writes for a reason, although he may not see it immediately, until one of his actions opens his eyes to it. I've always asked myself: what pushed me, for so many years, to wake up at dawn and work on this book? Only this morning I saw the reason.

When I first went to deposit the manuscript of this book, I took my daughter, Juilie, eight years old then, with me. On that day, the editor's office was under renovation. So we all sat there, surrounded by piles of books, and I glanced at Juilie. Her gaze, fixed upon the editor, radiated the same confidence I've seen, over and over, when I caught her spying on my clients. At that very moment, something clicked inside me, but I didn't understand its significance until today.

This morning, I woke up at 4:30, to finish the final touches on the manuscript. When I sat down at my desk, a fox howled in the forest behind our house, and the first train of the day rattled by on the tracks below my window. I rolled away from my desk and looked at the train. I imagined the same train taking us, me and Juilie, to the editor's office that day—my one hand on Juilie's shoulder, and the other holding the manuscript... And then I saw why I wrote this book.

I wrote it for my daughter—to return the confidence she placed upon me to heal others. Like every one of us, Juilie will enter into discordance with herself one day; it's an inevitable challenge the Universe places before *all* of us, for our growth. But, I may not be on this Earth then, to help her retrieve her balance. At that crucial moment of her life, this book will guide her through the challenges, as if I were at her side.

If that indeed happens, this book would have served its purpose.

Indrajit GARAI

5

Disclaimer

The approach of this book is strictly complementary to the modern medicine. If you have medical complications, your doctor's recommendations must prevail over this book.

The names and profiles of all characters are fictitious. To the best of my knowledge, they do not correspond to anyone particular from among my clients, alive or dead. Portrayed in fictional manner, they rather represent an imitation of the amalgam of personalities and problems I could encounter during my career. Any eventual similarities are entirely accidental and involuntary.

Unless associated with a male character, the masculine pronouns represent both genders.

1: Paving our way in

Listen to this conversation I had once with a client, before I wrote this book:

"Monsieur Garai, do you know why I hate those books on well-being?"

"No, I don't." I do want to know, though.

"Because their authors think they're smarter than us."

I stiffen. "Do they?"

"They believe they've gotten the life right, and the rest of us have it all wrong."

"Well…I never tell you what to do."

"But, you ask the right questions."

"How does that help?"

"They make me think. Then I find out, by myself, what's best for me."

"And that works?"

"Sure. One solution never fits all."

You've already tried methods of well-being, probably several. They impressed you, but they also ignored something unique about you. They worked, but only temporarily. Or, they still work, but only partially. The same methods have worked wonder for others— you've read in their testimonies. So, you think, there must be something wrong with you.

But, determined to procure a durable well-being, you continue your search. Because you know, the factors straining your well-being will keep growing, and eventually push you over the limits. Among all those methods available in the market, one has to work for you. You hurry, before it's too late.

You are not alone in this search.

For every one of us, life is changing by the day. Some thrive by taking these changes as challenges, by transforming uncertainties into opportunities, whereas others give in and sink in their self-esteem. Meanwhile, methods for being well and doing well keep proliferating further, in the bookstores and over the internet. Eight out of ten stare at this heap of methods and sigh: 'Should I have been born with *one* that works for me?'

Nevertheless, when I took a closer look at these people, I discovered something striking. *All* of them have been well and done well before, simply by their natural instincts. And then they lost it somehow.

That puzzle was the beginning of this book.

Then, from twelve years of working with clients, this is what I found. That *one* method, which works for you, originates from within you alone. In other words,

For lasting well-being, we must go for our original solution.

The reasons for this are the following:

- For a lasting well-being, we need accordance with our inner self,

- The peripheral solutions do not bring this accordance, but our original solution does,

- We can build our original solution easily, from inside out.

Our well-being envelops a context far larger than just management of stress at work. Well-being, here, refers to a frictionless functioning within the three spheres of our life:

- Our inner self;

- Our immediate surrounding, i.e., our family members, friends, and colleagues;

- And our external world, i.e., our casual acquaintances, and that unknown mass moving around us.

'The peripheral solutions' represent those one-to-one or group methods that address our signs of unwell-being piece by piece, from outside. Our 'original solution' takes its root within our core, and then proceeds outward—from the inner self, to the immediate surrounding, to the external world.

Part I shows why accordance with self is *the* most essential requirement for our well-being. What are the signs of 'accordance with self'? Why some arrive at this accordance gracefully, whereas others don't?

You dissect a method of well-being you've already undertaken in the past, and you discover what uniqueness in you went ignored; which aspects of the method appealed to you nevertheless, and what your responsibilities were for the suboptimal results. We try three techniques to approach our inner self, and you take a first shot at your original solution.

Part II shows why the peripheral solutions do not provide accordance with our self, but our original solution does. You build your own benchmarks. You discover how your physiological symptoms connect with your psychological ones, and how *both* evolve simultaneously with the intensity of your stress; how your qualities connect with your frailties; and how you can turn those frailties into qualities. In the light of these discoveries, you revise your original solution.

In part III, you implement your original solution systematically. You discover your 'constitution', i.e., your unique physical-cum-psychological makeup, and your personal triggers of stress. For your constitution, you learn to distinguish 'stress' from 'strain', and to decide when to intervene with corrective measures versus when to leave your organism alone.

You retrieve accordance with your self, refine your original solution, and reconstruct your well-being. You discover how to maintain your well-being, by 'living wholesome' in the three spheres of your life.

Your original solution is unique. This book does *not* provide you with a readymade solution. On the contrary, plenty of examples in this book guide you, step by step, in constructing *your* original solution.

Your unique solution comes from within you. You have fun constructing this solution. Along the process, you get to know yourself, accept yourself, and value yourself.

Your original solution remains dynamic, just like you. You learn to adapt it to the unique course of your evolution. This evolutionary awareness kicks the monotony out of your life, and you keep forging ahead with dignity.

So, let's go for it now.

Part I

For lasting well-being, we need accordance with our inner self

2: Poll shows well-being needs accordance with self

'What do you require for being well?' I asked my clients.

Among them, 67% replied, in one form or another: 'To be myself. To act by my principles.'

Another 29% indicated: 'To do only a few things, but do them really well.' For them, having too many things on their shoulders meant sacrificing quality, and the internal conflict that resulted from this compromise prevented them from feeling well within. In other words, these people also felt better when they could stick to *their* own standards of excellence.

The remaining 4% felt good only during vacations, alone. In addition to professional discordance, they had matters in their private lives that didn't go with who they were inside.

None of these people wanted, as the first requirement, to eliminate poor digestion, insomnia, anger, melancholy, or other usual symptoms of not being well. On the contrary, all their spontaneous responses converged upon 'fitting matters rightly inside.' This internal fit, deep into the self, came out as the most essential requirement for well-being.

Did these people refer only to their psychological well-being?
No.

Although none made a direct connection between body and mind, the essence of their responses showed that their physical state moved closely with their psychological state. And their global well-being emerged from their accordance with self—a tangible state within, characterized by distinctive feelings.

How do we feel 'accordance with self' in concrete terms?
"I feel in accordance with myself when I do what feels right for me," says Cecil, 33 years old, client director of a multinational consulting company. "Like, I've formed a team with myself."

"How do you know what feels right for you?" I ask.

"I watch my internal resistance. If I feel absolutely none, no matter how hard I work, I know I'm doing something that's right for me."

"And how do you feel after you finish?"

"A great relaxation. All over me, and deep inside me."

"In your private life, does it happen the same way?"

"Yes, absolutely. In a right relation, with friends or family, I feel no resistance from within. I may not talk a lot, but it just feels right." She leans over my desk. "Deep water doesn't splash, Monsieur Garai."

"What do you mean?"

"My inner self lies at my depth, right?" She places her palm on the chest. "To move with my self, first I've to reach that depth inside."

She sits erect at the edge of her seat. "When I reach that depth and find that accordance, I glide through life, without any friction. No bangs, no tussles, no rubbing—within me, or with anyone outside. Everything moves, in and out, in complete harmony."

"Even the things outside? You perceive them moving in harmony when—"

"When I'm in accordance with myself. Yes, that's how it feels."

"What gives you that perception?"

"These." She lifts her glasses. "When I have that accordance inside me, I look at the world through these lenses of accordance."

The same discussion, with three other long-term clients, showed similar characteristics of 'accordance with self':

- No resistance from inside,
- No friction with anyone outside,
- A deep and durable feeling of well-being,
- A perception of harmony all around.

When we have no frictions with ourselves, we have no frictions with anyone else; when we perceive harmony within ourselves, we also perceive harmony among others.

Our internal state influences our perceptions, thus our actions and reactions.

Accordance characterizes well-being. What characterizes unwell-being?

I asked my clients to portray their unwell-being.

Among them, 91% named a collection of symptoms: 'poor vital energy', 'poor digestion', 'insufficient sleep', 'repressed anger', 'perpetual sadness'…

Not *one* of them mentioned a misfit within.

The prefix 'un' before 'well' did something more than just negation—it pulled them away from their self within. Their perception changed. They started seeing disintegration within themselves, their body and mind separated from their self.

The remaining 9% defined a more concrete form of unwell-being:

"Some days just feel grey," says Patricia, 42 years old, managing director of an accounting firm, mother of two children, with a supportive husband.

"Grey?"

"Oh, you know what I mean." Her index and thumb make a zero. "When nothing feels right. And everything looks hazy."

"Let's be more specific."

"Neither excited, nor depressed. Neither at my best, nor at my worst. Neither pessimist, nor optimist…" Her head sinks in between her shoulders.

"You mean, like in limbo?"

"Yes!" She startles. "Just stuck in the middle. In a haze of mediocrity." Her eyes glaze. "Caught in a place I don't really belong to."

"How does such a day move for you?"

"That's the problem, Monsieur Garai." She sighs. "Nothing moves on a grey day. You wake up, and you don't feel good about yourself. You become irritated with your children, then with people in the metro. All this, for no reason." She shrugs. "At work, you pick on others. If that fails, you go mad with the weather."

"I see what you mean."

"I don't think you do." Her face twitches. "On a grey day, everything looks so boring, so annoying, so pointless…" She shakes her head. "All I see around me is… a bunch of obstacles."

"To what?"

"To going someplace worthy, Monsieur Garai. To doing something meaningful with my life." She glares around. "Those obstacles just stand in my way."

"Let's take a step back. Do your grey days always start by not feeling well within?"

"Yes, always." She clutches the corner of my desk. "I noticed that, since you asked me to. First, for no reason, my temper rots." She bites her lip. "Then, the rotten temper stinks outward—to my family, to my colleagues, to any Tom Dick Harry on the road."

She lifts her eyebrows. "The grey just hovers over me, Monsieur Garai. Hangs around me like a cloud of unbeatable flying pests."

Two other clients gave me similar responses. Overall, this group also recognized that their unwell-being originated from within.

The key to our well-being lies inside us, within our inner self.

We'll get hold of this key.

Exercise 1: Your first approach to your inner self

Close your eyes, and visualize your latest episode of panic.

Let your body react to this memory. Observe how your respiration and heartbeats speed up, but don't force them to calm down. Observe how your thoughts bombard inside you, but do not try to stop them.

Now, watch the sensations in your belly, back, hands, legs…the changes of temperature inside you. Note your emotions, but don't label them as frustration, anger, guilt, regret, or anxiety…. Just observe how these sensations and emotions diffuse through your body, but do no more.

Give your mind a free rein. Let it wander into the supermarket, into the bank, into your child's room, into your office… Don't force any direction. Just observe simply.

***

How did you feel during this exercise?

- Your physical discomforts eased away slowly,

- Your emotions lost their intensity gradually,

- And blanks appeared in between your thoughts.

Overall, you feel refreshed now, possibly, more vigorous than before. The memory of your panic may still linger, but it looks much smaller than you.

What happened inside you during this exercise?

You didn't steer your body or mind anywhere. You just observed them, and they took care of themselves. We shall enter into the mechanics of this exercise in part III, but, for now, let's understand globally how this exercise works over panic.

When panic strikes, something disconnects inside you; your body and mind, both, run their separate ways. This dissociation happens at the level that envelops both, but you get caught up in controlling them separately.

The exercise you just did shows this envelope has a mechanism of auto-correction. When we allow this mechanism a free rein, the envelope restores its equilibrium all by itself.

This envelope represents your inner self. It encompasses your body and mind; it also constitutes them both, as their primary ingredient. When you let your mechanism of auto-regulation free, your body and mind move in accordance with this envelope.

We won't define this 'inner self' any further. Rather, through the remaining exercises in this book, we'll feel it intuitively, and reactivate its mechanism of auto-correction.

"Our inner self is something we can't understand logically," says Christine, 59 years old, an entrepreneur. "But, to achieve accordance with this self, we have to get hold of it first, somehow."

"How did you get hold of yours?"

"By plucking all those leeches." She pinches the skin of her forearm. "Once I wrenched those blood-suckers off me, I could feel my self again."

"Did your attitude change too?"

"Oh, yes!" She leans back. "I became a lot gentler." She scratches the glass-top of my desk. "I don't oppress myself to death anymore. Nor do I squeeze others in a vise."

"Did you go away somewhere, to do all that?"

"No, Monsieur Garai." She flings her hand over the head. "I didn't go to the mountains, or to the oceans. I did all this right here,"—her index points to the floor—"in this urban swamp."

You can do that too.

3: Methods that don't provide accordance produce transient results

'Why do the methods of well-being lose their appeal?' I asked my clients.

Everyone I asked had tried one method of well-being, at least a group method provided by their employers, but gave up somewhere between two and five months. Even the most entertaining methods lost their appeal.

The three cases below, chosen from the three spheres of life — the inner self, the immediate surrounding, and the external world — show where the thread of appeal went severed.

Case Study: within self

Lionel, 38 years old, rock singer, now sees a relaxation therapist for his pangs of anxiety.

After having swallowed tranquilizers for eight years, he decided to change psychiatrist. His new psychiatrist stopped all medications, and referred him to this relaxation therapist, but relaxation hasn't helped Lionel either.

"These damn peaks of anxiety!" Lionel flicks lint from the cuff of his sleeve. "They come every time I start working on a new song."

"Do they come before you start rehearsing?"

"No! No! I'm fine once I get going with the song." His forehead creases. "The anxiety comes *before* I write the song. To be precise, a couple of days before."

"Then what happens?"

"The song flows out of my pen, and all anxieties disappear." He exhales. "But those days, just before writing, are honestly unbearable." He flicks lint from the other cuff. "I end up doing crazy things."

"Did you say all these to your relaxation therapist?"

"Yes." His eyes narrow. "She said, 'You've to stop your anxiety right away, before it gets out of your hands.' But, how?" His nose flares. "She said, 'Use breathing exercises.' But, that stupid breathing stuff won't work for me at all!"

"How long have you been trying her exercises?"

"Oaf! Couple of times may be." His shoulders rise and fall. "They work better on others. She is a great teacher though."

"Why do you think these exercises don't work for you?"

"My problem is…hmm…" He rubs his thumb on the palm. "I don't like running away from anxiety. Not really." His eyes sparkle. "My best songs you know,"—he spreads his arms—"I wrote my best songs at the worst moments of my life."

"Anxiety precedes your creativity then?"

"Yes."

"Maybe, anxiety is the source of your creativity."

He startles. "The source?" Then a smile stretches the corners of his mouth. "You could say anxiety is part of my creativity. But, the anxiety also handicaps me, I mean sometimes."

"How?"

"Well, the anxiety is there always, before I write a song. Only sometimes, it gets out of my hands." His eyes lower. "When I went to see this therapist, all I really wanted was to reduce its intensity."

"What happened then?"

"She gave me a routine of breathing exercises. A routine, she said, she gives to all anxious people." He slides the tips of his fingers along the collar of his shirt. "Honestly, I've tried those exercises, and they stress me to death. I'm better off living with my anxiety."

"You aren't really convinced you want to get rid of your anxiety."

"I think, if I got rid of it completely, I'll hurt my creativity. Most feel anxious before a race, don't they?"

"Yes, they do."

"Then, why should the race of creativity be an exception?" He rubs the pulps of his fingers. "Well, it won't hurt me though, to reduce the intensity a bit."

"That's where those breathing exercises come in, Lionel."

"I told you,"—he whistles—"they won't work for me."

"They'll work, as long as they fit with your attitude toward anxiety."

"Fit with my attitude toward anxiety?" His eyebrows rise. "Now, you're losing me."

"You value your anxiety, Lionel. You should do those exercises *not* to stop your anxiety, but to keep it within a bound, a manageable range. So the anxiety doesn't kill the creativity it brings."

He scratches his beard. "What should I do then?"

"Master those exercises first, whole-heartedly. Then personalize them. Adapt them in a way that suits you the best. All along, maintain your attitude toward anxiety, the way you see it as your friend. Find a solution that works for *you*."

"Oh, no! I don't have time for all that." The skin furrows between his eyebrows. "I'm already paying her a fortune to do all this for me."

Case Study: within immediate surrounding

Elizabeth, 43 years old, Adjunct Director of Human Resources in an investment bank, doesn't like to go to a lot of meetings. She joined the company four years ago as compensation manager, and has moved up to this position since. Her new boss, an external recruit, sent her to a seminar on effective communication.

Elizabeth has completed this workshop, but with a lot of grudges.

"I don't like to raise an avalanche of words." She locks her fingers over the lap. "I like to listen instead, and then lead with questions. The right questions, so the person before me can find the right answer, by herself."

"Do the employees come to see you often?"

"I would say, yes." Her fingers unlock. "With financial markets so turbulent these days, many executives need a little pat on their backs."

"They take up a lot of your time. And that's what bothers your boss?"

"Yes." Her head cants. "But, counseling employees is one of the fundamental roles of human resources. A rather important one."

She tucks her chin in. "We shouldn't just go to meetings, hire people, compensate them somehow, as long as we need them, and then throw them out on the streets. We have to treat our employees like humans, not just resources."

"You find you add more value in those one-to-one meetings with employees."

"Not just in the one-on-one meetings, Monsieur Garai." Her chin juts toward me. "I also know how to get my messages across during group meetings." She sniffs. "And I can do that without thumping over the table, or yelling at others."

"You feel communicating that way is not in your blood."

She nods. "Of course, my colleagues got a lot more out of that workshop than I did. For me, all those howling and growling show only the void inside, only the insecurity. You know what?" Her pupils constrict. "Now, I even dislike the job I used to enjoy before."

"Did you discuss all this with your workshop trainer?"

"Oh, yes." She crosses her arms over the chest. "He said, 'Speak up, Elizabeth. That's what your boss wants you to do.' Like that was a surprise to me."

"Looks like, that workshop didn't motivate you."

"Not at all."

"Did you learn something new from that workshop?"

"No." Her hands clasp the biceps. "Nothing new."

"That doesn't sound like you, Elizabeth."

"Really?" Her hands drop on her lap. "May be…" Her lips curl. "Well, I learnt how to structure messages better. That part was great, but who said I've to get louder to do that? Or, drown others under my words?"

"I agree, you don't have to."

"Then how do I…"

"Retain your natural communication style. And then combine it with their method of structuring messages. Your delivery will gain a lot more power."

"But that's *not* what my boss wants." She stamps her foot. "He wants me to speak more, and louder, and go to more meetings—" The handbag falls off her lap.

"Does your boss appreciate the rapport you have with the employees?"

"Yes." She picks up her bag and zips it. "He certainly does, he has told me that."

"He values you, Elizabeth. Otherwise, he wouldn't have cared to send you to that workshop."

Her eyes lower. "But, he and I have such different views on communication."

"Exactly." I lean forward. "Why don't you make a lunch appointment with your boss? Explain to him, in a relaxed environment, that you understand his point. But, by going too far out of your natural style, you'll hurt your own performance. And, eventually, the performance of the entire team."

She gapes. "You must be joking, Monsieur Garai. If I do that, I'll get immediately marked as someone too different. Things don't work that way within our company."

"The differences you have with your boss may be complementary, not contradictory. It will be worth giving a try."

"No!"

She lifts her handbag and puts it in between us.

Case Study: within external world

Sarah, 28 years old, high school teacher, moved to a big city from a small village. Her husband, executive in consumer industries, has been promoted from the company's warehouse to its headquarters.

The change has been harsh for Sarah. To cope with it, she has joined a support group that helps people adjust to the city life, but each meeting with this group has made her feel only a little worse than before.

"My husband and our two children have no problems adjusting here." Her boot clacks against the leg of her chair. "Why can't I get over my blues?"

"What bothers you in this city?"

"What bothers me?" Her eyebrows rise in a sharp angle. "The aggression, the injustice, the insensitivity..." She taps her knuckles on my desk. "Am I telling you anything new, Monsieur Garai? No. Just inhumane here. And disgusting."

"What do you do in your support group?"

"Drills of compassion," — her nose crinkles — "simulated compassion, of course. Then I go out, try those lessons on others, and they just blow up like this." Her palm stops inches from her face.

"You're bothered people don't return your compassion."

"Come on, Monsieur Garai!" The sinews of her throat stiffen. "Isn't that the minimum one should expect in return? They tell us in our group, 'To receive compassion, start by giving it.'" Her head tilts backward. "Do you ever read philosophy?"

"Sometimes."

"Remember the philosopher that called animals 'animated objects'?" She shakes her head. "Surely, he didn't look at the people in this city. If he did, he would have called them 'unanimated souls'."

"People may look passive, even unapproachable sometimes. But that doesn't mean—"

"Unapproachable? Have you ever looked at their faces?" She puckers her lips. "Does that give you the desire to approach them? The grimaces, the frowns, the corners of their mouth down…"

"I know, I know. But that's not because they're judging you. Their facial expressions reflect what's going on inside them: conflicts, sufferings—"

"Exactly!" She claps. "And guilt, and misery…" She counts on her fingers. "If Victor Hugo lived today, he would have written another book called 'Les Nouveaux Miserables'."

"Many of these people could be in the same boat as you. They also might have moved from—"

"Stop! I don't want to be in the same boat with them."

"What do you want to do then?"

"Monsieur Garai." A long sigh blows out of her. "I don't know what I should do. If I did, I wouldn't come to you. All I'm saying is…it's not my fault."

Her shoulders sag. "But this support group makes me feel like it's my fault. They ask me to have compassion for those miserable people, and I can't. As a result,"—she chokes—"I feel oppressed. From inside, and out."

In the cases above, the methods failed not because something was wrong with them, but because how the trainers and the trainees chose to apply them. Both were responsible for the sub-optimal results.

The trainers ignored something unique inside the trainees:

- Lionel's anxiety stimulates his creativity,

- Elizabeth's personal style anchors her success,

- Sarah's compassion comes with an expectation of return.

The trainees ignored their own responsibilities too:

- Lionel believed personalization didn't merit his time,

- Elizabeth didn't risk being different from the rest,

- Sarah shifted the burden of her problem on others.

Four out of five failures arise from such personal factors.

Exercise 2: Identify the problem at its source

Choose one method you have undertaken in the past. List, on a fresh sheet, using complete sentences:

- Your uniqueness that you believe went ignored by your trainer,

- The aspects of the method that nevertheless appealed to you,

- Your own responsibilities, as you perceive, in obtaining the sub-optimal result.

Exercise 3: Your second approach to your inner self

Sit up straight. Place your relaxed hands on your thighs. For each hand, bring the tips of index and thumb together, with a light but firm pressure. Close your eyes, and don't move.

In a few seconds, you'll feel pulsations at the points of contact. Note that the pulsations are a bit stronger in one hand than the other.

What is the relation between this exercise and our inner self?
Two meridians pass through our arms to the fingertips. Our vital energy pulsates through these meridians. Depending on the energetic state of our organism, one of these meridians dominates: during stress, the right dominates; during rest, the left. That's why, through our digital pulses, we can feel the energetic state of our inner self.

This dominance shifts, spontaneously, every two hours. This cyclic shift represents the automatic regulation of our organism, by the balancing counteractive forces within us, but we are unconscious of all these happening inside. We can, however, influence this cycle to some extent, through conscious efforts, particularly during high stress.

Now, let's take this experiment a step further.

Feel your pulses again, but, this time, pay attentions to the tiny variations of their rhythms. Just wish, gently, that these pulsations become equal for both hands, but don't move, nor change the pressure on your fingertips.

What did you feel?
- The frequency of your thoughts fell,
- Your sensorial awareness heightened,

- Your pulses became equal for both hands.

With only a few days of regular practice, we can influence the cyclic dominance of the digital pulses at our will; thus, we can use the natural balancing mechanism of our body to our advantage during stress.

Let's not assume, however, that all stress is bad for us. We'll discuss the benefits of stress in part III, but, for the moment, let's remember what we saw with Lionel: some stress is inevitable, if we want to bring any creativity to our work. Contrary to the popular belief, this stress actually boosts the health of our organism. Call it 'good stress' if you like, but our organism needs it, to bring the best out of us. What we really want is to keep this beneficial stress within a bound, so it doesn't burn the creativity it brings along. That's where the exercise above comes to our help.

Use this exercise for prevention
As stress rises, the cyclic shift occurs more frequently, to balance our organism more effectively. During periods of intense stress, every two or three hours, take a couple of minutes to feel your digital pulses. This awareness itself dissolves your excessive stress, brings it down to a manageable level, and repairs your organism's damage.

This awareness has a preventive value too. As you come closer to your inner self, you feel rooted within, and you act in coherence with your deepest values. This coherence reduces your internal conflicts; your terrain generates less stress from within;

consequently, the stress from outside can't oppress you easily. Overall, you become more robust to stress.

This heightened awareness is the prerequisite for making your method of well-being work in accordance with you. When you sharpen this consciousness, you become capable of not only choosing a method that feels right for you, but also combining it with the best inside you, and then constructing a solution that works for you the best.

And that becomes your original solution.

4: Methods that provide accordance produce durable results

In this chapter we'll see how, in accordance with our self, we can personalize the methods of well-being to fit our unique needs, and how we can adapt these methods to the unique course of our evolution.

Case Study

Beatrice, 34 years old, takes a month off between jobs, and goes to a conference for well-being. She calls me one evening:

"I've made a mistake coming here, Monsieur Garai. Their program weighs too much on me for vacation."

"What do you have there?"

"A lot." She sighs. "Stress management, nutrition, yoga…enough to stress me out."

"Can you choose?"

"Difficult." She smacks her lips. "All excellent professionals. I won't get this chance again."

"What do you do on a typical day?"

"That'll be hard to describe." Her voice fades. "A lot in groups, and then alone…"

"What's bothering you, Beatrice?"

"I don't appreciate how they treat stress here,"—she clears her throat—"like something deadly and contagious."

"They want you to keep stress out of your life?"

"Right. And I can't function without stress."

"Good stress, you mean?"

"Stress that motivates me."

"Then retain that mindset. And, participate in their workshops."

"That sounds contradictory, Monsieur Garai."

"Not at all. Do what they ask you to do, but don't soak up everything."

"With that attitude, will I learn anything?"

"To learn, you don't have to agree a hundred percent with your trainer. Keep your mind open, draw the best from them, and then build what suits *you* the best."

"That's a lot you're asking from me."

"You can do it. Try sincerely, and leave all criticisms out."

Example: How we can personalize our methods of well being

Two and a half months later, Beatrice comes to my office.

"After we spoke, I stopped judging them altogether." She leans back on her chair.

"What happened then?"

"I could learn a lot more from their trainings."

"Your mind became free and flexible."

"And I had so much energy!" She puckers her lips. "I paid for my criticisms, though."

"How?"

"When I criticized too much, people just went away from me."

"Why?"

"I guess, they thought…I might criticize them too, before others."

"What else did you learn there?"

"How to separate real priorities from the illusive ones." The corner of her mouth twists. "Well, their program didn't teach me that, directly. It surfaced within me, when I let that pressure go."

"Can you elaborate?"

"There was a lot to do. So I prioritized my tasks, and then started with the one I had the most control over." She raises her eyebrows. "My list of tasks, even there, was a hundred kilometers long."

"Why?"

"I wanted to do what everyone else did."

"Those were not *your* priorities then."

She dips her head. "Right."

"Did you shorten your list?"

"That was the surprise, Monsieur Garai." Her eyes sparkle. "When I took that social pressure off, the list shortened by itself!"

"You chose to listen to your heart."

"Finally." She inflates her cheeks and blows. "A lot fell off my list, and a lot more went to the bottom."

"What did you do about those at the bottom?"

"Nothing." She scratches her cheek. "They sorted out by themselves."

"You let them?"

"I had absolutely no control over those, anyway." She brings her hair over the shoulder and starts braiding. "So why worry about them?"

"What does that say about priorities?"

She stops braiding. "They are tasks we can do something about."

"Tell me about your other programs there."

She pushes her hair back and sits upright. "They gave us great recipes, for anything and everything to do with stress." She smacks her lips. "The only problem is—you spend so much time looking for those ingredients. And, cooking their complicated recipes."

"What do you do differently?"

"Unless I'm sick, I eat what's natural and tasty. In small quantities."

"You let your tongue guide you."

"It's the excess that kills, Monsieur Garai. Excess, even in the best quality food, would kill a healthy person in the long term. Sadly, foods no longer feed our physical hunger. They fulfill our emotional famine instead. What a pity it—"

"You must have learnt something there. You had an open mind after all."

"Ah, yes. One nutritionist introduced the notion of incompatibility. Unfortunately, others became so obsessed with nutritional values of foods, she just skipped the subject of incompatibility altogether."

"But, it made sense to you."

"Intuitively, a lot. You can eat a great dish, made from a lot of great stuff. But, if the ingredients don't go well together, you digest nothing."

"Did you discuss this with that nutritionist?"

"I would have, but she had left. So I researched her concept later, in the library. Guess what? Some really interesting combinations came up."

"Give me an example."

"Mix dairy products with orange juice, as we often do in breakfast. Nothing is digested. On top of that, you get acid, when the juice curdles the milk."

"What happens when you get acid everyday?"

"Ulcers. Arthritis, when the blood becomes too acid."

"Any other combinations that you think don't go together?"

"I don't think ice-cream goes with cola. Cheese with meat neither. Imagine what would happen if you had all four of them together?" She traces a ball over her belly. "Since I stopped mixing these, my stomach doesn't bloat anymore. Nor do I feel drowsy after meals."

Let's step aside for a moment. Improper food habits, such as incompatible mixes or enormous quantities, have more consequences than just bloating our stomach, or making us drowsy after meals:

Our stomach is a pouch of muscles; they stretch when we eat. If our stomach bloats after every meal, from fermentation of incompatible mixes or from large quantities of food, its size increases slowly. An oversized stomach suffocates the spleen behind, and blocks the circulation of vital energy in its meridian.

The spleen meridian separates the good parts of the food from its waste. Perturbation in this meridian causes poor digestion and loose stool.

By producing lymphocytes, the spleen reinforces our immunity. Poor energy in the spleen means poor energy for the lymphocytes, which means poor immunity.

Perturbation of the spleen meridian also perturbs sleep; we wake up around 3 am.

There are biomechanical consequences of increasing the stomach size too. During respiration, the oversized stomach prevents the diaphragm from descending properly into the abdominal cavity, and massaging efficiently the other organs there. These organs congest, and their functions degrade.

Shallow movements of the diaphragm bring in less oxygen per breath. To compensate, the frequency of respiration has to increase. This can happen only if the respiratory centers, inside the hypothalamus and the medulla oblongata, accelerate their rhythm. But this acceleration also increases our susceptibility to stress.

Moreover, a bloated stomach exerts pressure on the intestines, and on other organs in the pelvic cavity, such as urinary and reproductive ones. Their disorders develop.

Let's return to Beatrice.

"What else did you learn there?"

"The yoga classes were oppressive." She pats her chest. "But, there was one teacher who did one-to-one consultations. I found his method suited me the best."

"What was different about his method?"

"He said: 'In yoga, your only reference is yourself'. That fits my philosophy a lot better." She opens a notebook, and stops at a page-mark.

I lean forward.

"Before, those premenstrual syndromes drove me nuts." She clears her throat. "This teacher explained, in simple terms, how the menstrual system works." She taps on a page with anatomical drawings. "Then he showed me which postures would help, and why."

She closes the notebook and tucks it away. "He also explained the close connection between the ovaries and the thyroid. Which postures would help my thyroid and, through it, my ovaries."

"Have you tried those postures before?

"Yes, but blindly." She prunes her lips. "Now that I know how they work, I obtain far better results than before."

"Why do you think that knowledge improved your results?"

"For something to work for me, I have to understand it first."
She touches her temple. "Thoroughly. That goes with who I am."

"Can we return to your teacher's point on reference?"

"I know what you're going to say, Monsieur Garai." She
beams. "When I'm doing yoga, if I go too far beyond my natural
limits, I not only hurt my joints and tendons, but also increase my
stress."

Let's step aside again and see why, in yoga, going too far beyond
our natural limits hurts us more than helping.

When we take yogic stretches far beyond our natural limits,
the resulting pain stimulates a group of receptors embedded in the
extremities of our muscle tendons, and activates a defensive
mechanism to protect us. If we ignore this mechanism and force our
stretch too much, we end up causing permanent damages to our
joints, tendons, and ligaments.

Via neuromuscular pathways, these pain receptors also relay
signals of emergency to our brain. In response, the brain instructs the
adrenal glands to secrete adrenaline, the hormone of emergency. But,
this adrenaline isn't used up fully in such pseudo-emergencies,
provoked by painful stretches. The unused adrenaline maintains a
state of diluted stress inside us, long after the yoga session has
finished. Consequently, we feel edgy for the rest of the day, and we
can't sleep well at night.

Adrenaline also leaves residues on our blood vessels and
nerves. This makes them degenerate over the long term.

How far should we stretch in yoga?

We get the maximum benefit from yoga as long as we engage our muscles and organs near our natural limits, i.e., at a point where we can hold the stretches, comfortably, for several minutes.

Our optimal point of engagement depends not only on our flexibility, but also on our morphology. That's why this point of engagement is unique for every one of us.

And, that's why: In yoga, your only reference is *you*.

While we execute any yogic protocol, we should take the posture to the limit of our stretch, so our deep muscles and organs engage. And then release the stretch slightly, so we can hold the posture without stress for two to three minutes. During this hold, we should breathe deeply but smoothly. This stimulates our muscles and organs, increases their blood circulation, and enhances their neural currents.

The health of our entire organism improves.

Some of us see yoga as pure stretching, where we struggle to bring two extremities together, e.g., when we try to touch the toes while keeping the legs straight, thereby creating a feeling of stress and compression within. There, a complete change of perspective becomes necessary:

Instead of fighting to bring the two extremities together, we should visualize ourselves extending from our navel, toward the two extremities we're trying to meet. At the same time, we should also visualize ourselves expanding outward, through deep but smooth

42

breathing. This sensation, of extending and expanding simultaneously, gives us the feel of having more space within—something we all need, particularly when sandwiched between stress from inside and outside.

This simple change of perspective takes all stress out of the practice of yoga.

Example: How we can fit our personalized methods to our evolution

A year and a half later, Beatrice returns to my office.

"That workshop served as my stepping stone." She rubs her hands. "I've evolved since, and my methods have evolved with me."

"Give me an example."

"I saw, it's not just what I eat, but how I eat *also* matters."

"What do you do differently now?"

"I no longer eat at my desk. I've cut all stress out of my meals, and I digest a lot better since then."

"That's a great leap in nutrition!"

"And I no longer do yoga like a robot." She slides her hand over the abdomen. "Now I skip a day or two. Go walking, swimming, cycling…or simply do nothing. The results still last."

"How?"

"I think, when people don't obsess with a method, they extract a lot more from it."

"Why?"

"Methods are only means to a goal, right? The goal here is well-being. But, some of us get so obsessed with perfecting our methods, that we lose sight of that goal."

"What happens to our evolution then?"

"You still evolve, I guess." She shifts. "But in the wrong direction. Anyway, when you're obsessed with methods, you can't see your evolution."

"What happens to those methods then?"

"They bore you." She shivers. "You give up."

"Did you see *your* evolution?"

She startles. "Yes, always." Her chin touches the sternum. "And that saved me from so much trouble."

"What kind of trouble?"

"Before, I would chase, non-stop, whatever new came along my way." Her eyebrows rise and fall. "But, when I saw my evolution, I gave up that futile chase."

"You saw the *new* in you."

"Yes." She sits upright. "There's always something new in me." Her fingers drum on the desk. "Toward what I'm evolving, I don't know, but I don't care anymore."

"Now you trust your instincts more."

She nods. "I know they'll take me in the direction I want to go."

"Do others see you differently?"

"Yes. But, I haven't done anything special for them to see me differently."

"Then, how did that happen?"

"When I saw my evolution, I saw myself more positively. So, others do the same, I guess."

"What else have you noticed?"

"I have absolutely no conflict inside me today." She leans on the backrest. "I work better with others. What more can we expect, Monsieur Garai?"

Eight out of ten, who took time to personalize their methods, with awareness of their evolution, reported similar results.

Exercise 4: Your first step toward your original solution
Take your worksheet from the last chapter, and another fresh sheet.

Is there something *you* felt particularly ignored about you, by your trainer?

Yes. Then, that's your zone of unique sensitivity.

What's so special about this zone?

It's also the source of your unique strengths.

Now, trust your intuition, and value those unique strengths of yours. Then, with this boosted confidence in yourself, write down:

- How you'll combine your unique strengths with those parts of the method that appealed to you. *You've just taken the first step toward your original solution.*

- What adjustments you'll make in your attitude, to implement this solution efficiently and effectively? *You've just made a great leap in your evolution.*

Don't worry about perfecting the details right now. Throughout this book, you'll refine your original solution several times.

Exercise 5: Your third approach to your inner self

Pick up a book.

As you read through, underline those few words that stand out flagrantly to you. After you've finished the book, write those words on a clean sheet, with at least two centimeters of space in between.

Next day, glance at those words, without fixating on any of them specifically.

Together, what image do they bring up spontaneously?

Name that image, in concrete terms.

Do the same exercise for a dozen of books, without looking at the previous images. Use a separate sheet for each book, to mark the special words on.

Take those dozen sheets, and look at the constellation of their images.

Do you see the commonalities among them?

Yes. You've just discovered another part of your inner self.

Later, go a step further: while you continue this exercise, notice how your perceptions of external events, and your reactions to them, evolve.

If you do not love books, replace them by paintings, or songs, or any other artistic works.

Part II

The peripheral solutions don't bring accordance, but our original solution does

5: Peripheral solutions operate on external benchmarks

In part I, we saw what 'accordance with self' means, and why this accordance is a crucial requirement for lasting well-being. We also saw how blind pursuit of general methods leads to transient well-being at the best, whereas personalization of these methods leads to permanent well-being via accordance with self.

The general methods, not adapted to the specific needs of an individual, remain peripheral, i.e., they address only those problems that manifest at the surface of an individual. In this part, we delve deeper into why these peripheral solutions fail to provide accordance with our self, but our original solutions succeed.

The methods in this part have a significant difference with those we have seen previously. In part I, we looked only into the group methods, which leave little margins for the trainer and the trainee to personalize them. In this part, we'll look into one-to-one methods that, in spite of a higher scope for personalization, end up peripheral, thus fail to provide accordance with self.

Why do such methods end up peripheral?
For three main reasons:
- They base themselves on external benchmarks,
- They fix problems one by one,
- They ignore the connection between quality and frailty.

In this chapter, we explore the first reason.

Case Study

Stephan, 42 years old, has joined a job in Environmental Engineering, after a professional reorientation. His wife took an appointment with me, for him.

"You look fine, Stephan. What's bothering you?"

"I sleep five to six hours a night." He avoids my gaze.

"So?"

"That bothers my wife." He turns his eyes toward me.

I see no dark circles under his eyes, nor any pouches. His face muscles don't twitch. He feels my eyes on him, and crosses his arms.

"Do you feel drowsy? Or, restless?"

"God no!" He frowns. "My new job is so exciting." His arms uncross. "I don't have time for that kind of stuff."

"How many hours did you sleep before?"

"Bof! At least nine. Sometimes, eleven." He places his hands over the knees. "My former job was dead boring. I hibernated there for seven years."

"Does your wife see your enthusiasm now?"

"She certainly does. We make…hmm…" He bites his lip. "She read in a book: 'If you sleep less than eight hours a night, you must be ill.'" His eyes avert. "So, I'm here."

"What does your doctor say?"

"He sees no problem with my health." His nose crinkles. "But my wife keeps giving me all these plant-based remedies for insomnia."

"You don't like those plants?"

"I would have, if they made any difference. The only thing they do," —he grimaces— "give me nausea. Honestly, they put a brake on my enthusiasm."

"Tell me about your current assignment."

"We're developing the blueprint for an ecological garbage disposal site. Really exciting stuff!"

"Your patience is paying off now."

"And my hard works too. For two years, I took evening classes, sacrificed all social events, spent almost no time with my family on the weekends. You're right. All that work is paying off now."

"Your enthusiasm drags you out of bed, before you complete eight hours."

"Yes." His eyebrows rise and fall. "And then I get my first cocktail of plants."

"When did you start those plants?"

"Two weeks ago." His jaws tighten. "I'm doing perfectly fine with five-six hours of sleep. I have so much energy—at work, at home... My last job was a prison for me." His arms hang limp. "I didn't feel like leaving the bed. I had energy for nothing."

"That's behind you now. How is your appetite these days?"

"Normal. At last!" He blows. "Before, I munched chips and sipped colas all day long. Lapped up a gallon of coffee per day. At home, I would eat meals for ten—"

"Stephan, how do you eat *now*?"

"Now? I eat fine. And I do sports on the weekends again. Finally I've lost all those kilos, around here." He circles his hand over the belly.

"Changing job helped your metabolism."

"What? Metabolism?"

"Changing job helped you lose weight."

"I think it did. But my wife thinks it's those plants that shed my weight."

"Why did you come to see me?"

"Why? Because my wife said, I must see you. And be patient. Frankly—"

"Frankly, you don't need me, Stephan. When you're happy, your organism gets by with less food and less sleep."

We'll return later to the link between humor, appetite, and sleep. For now, let's focus on the main point of this chapter. Stephan's wife used those plant-based remedies by an external benchmark: 'minimum eight hours of sleep is a must for *all* healthy adults.'

Let's not forget that insufficient sleep does weaken the nervous, endocrinal, and immune systems. Other pathological signs such as vertigo, troubled speech and vision, and irritable humor accompany chronic insomnia. Medical help must be sought in such cases. Nevertheless, the issue of insomnia, in most healthy adults, is exaggerated today.

At a centre for Sports Therapy and Natural Medicine, we did a study on self-reported insomniacs, i.e., people who, with no other illness, thought they didn't sleep enough. Of them, 93% admitted that their insomnia was exaggerated by friends, colleagues, or stray magazine articles.

If you're a healthy person, your amount and pattern of sleep stay unique. Relying on external benchmarks, as in the case of Stephan, creates havoc on your mind first, and then on your body. Your natural efficiency diminishes as a result.

Sleep is not our only biological indicator that's under social attack.

Frequently, the peer pressure for happiness and libido is so high, and so contagious, that people ignore their own feelings altogether, and think they never have enough. Below, I show the main concern in 782 people of sound health:

- 44% complained of lack of sleep

- 38%, of lack of libido

- 18%, of lack of perpetual joy

All these people have built their benchmarks of sleep, libido, and joy based solely upon what they hear from others, completely ignoring what they've observed about themselves, when they were going well. Moreover, most of these people have accepted the largest of these figures in each category as the standard of good health. As a result, they have mistrusted their own biological indicators, and seriously devalued their health.

We've just seen how Stephan does fine with five to six hours of sleep per night. In chapter 3, we saw mood swings were part of

Lionel's creativity. Jean-Paul, baker at a world-famous pastry shop, deals with external benchmarks this way:

"Imagine what will happen if I slept ten hours every night, made love four times daily, and stayed high the rest of the day?"

"What will happen?"

"Who would bake the pastries?" His head tilts backward. "I get up every dawn at four, even on Sunday."

"You could go to sleep at eight."

"My kids eat dinner at eight."

"Hmm…That could be a problem."

"And my wife doesn't get in bed before eleven." He winks. "And she gets crappy if we don't—"

"I get your point, Jean-Paul."

He clears his throat. "On grey days like this, that leaves us with only one alternative: stay high, all day long, on ecstasy." His voice lowers. "One dawn, I did bake my pastries on ecstasy. Guess what happened?"

"The queue wrapped around the block."

"No." He growls. "I never saw the same clients again."

"Oops."

"We need *all* emotions to make our life. The same way we need *all* tastes to make a good cake."

"Even the bitter taste?"

"Absolutely." His eyes open wide. "You can't make cakes without the bitter taste. What do you think chocolates taste like without sugar?"

"Jean-Paul, why do you think people complain of depression so often?"

"Because they think others are happier than them. They believe in all those lies others tell them."

"Have you ever taken—"

"Anti-depressants?" He grins. "Who hasn't taken that at least once?"

"What was the experience like?"

"Have you ever been your own phantom? Do you know what it feels like?"

"You prefer to be yourself."

"Sure, I prefer depression to anti-depressants."

"Are you in good health, Jean Paul?"

"Check my teeth." He opens his mouth. "Others might think I'm a nut, but do I look like a peanut?"

"Why peanut?"

"I'll tell you why." He leans forward on the elbows. "Sleep ten hours a night on pills, screw four times per day on aphrodisiacs, float on ecstasy all day long… and that's what you become, Monsieur: a peanut." He smacks his lips. "People tramp on you, and you crack."

For a healthy person, the rhythms of sleep, libido, and mood depend on his constitutional makeup. Changing these indicators, without paying regard to his overall health, causes severe damages to his constitution.

Exercise 6: Build your own benchmarks.

You have your unique rhythm of sleep, energy, and mood.

Over several weeks, note their variations, during periods of high motivation, and during low. You'll discover your unique pattern. If you consider any other indicators important for you particularly, such as appetite, note their variations as well. For example, you may notice:

- During periods of high motivation, you wake up around 5 am, your creativity peaks around 10 am, and your energy dips around 3 pm, and then rises again;

- During periods of low motivation, you wake up between 1 and 3 am, your mood stays low until 11 am, and your energy collapses around 8 pm, accompanied by melancholy or fear.

These are the rhythms of *your* biodynamic force, which is unique. Arising out of your constitutional makeup, these rhythms don't change a lot over your life.

Why learn these rhythms?

These rhythms benchmark, uniquely, your global internal state. They tell you when you should take corrective measures, and when you shouldn't.

Here, 'taking corrective measures' does *not* translate into consuming remedies separately for insomnia, bad mood, or low energy; rather, it translates into uncovering the discordance within you, at the root of *all* problems, and then finding your original solution that aligns accordance with self.

Save this worksheet on your rhythms. In part III, we'll use these indicators, to determine your constitutional makeup.

6: Peripheral solutions fix problems patch by patch

In the last chapter, we've seen how peripheral solutions, by operating on external benchmarks, create suboptimal targets.

In this chapter, we'll see how peripheral methods, by seeking separate solutions for problems with a common root, push us farther and farther away from well-being.

Almost always, they end up aggravating the cause at the root.

Case Study

Karen, 41 years old, financial trader, has been forced to work for a former subordinate, after two banks merged. She struts into my office. Her protruding jaw muscles and acrid breath announce repressed anger.

"Our relation turned hostile as soon as we started working together." She tosses her handbag on the sofa. "A month from then, I started having health issues."

"What type?"

"I would wake up with a rotten breath. Wouldn't feel like going to work. Whatever I ate for lunch, even a simple salad, would give me acid. I was irritable like hell, all the time, for no reason."

"Did you have skin eruptions?"

"Yes! Big red patches," — her fingers close in on her palm — "like a leopard."

"How was your sleep?"

"Woke up every night, in a pool of hot sweat. Had violent nightmares. In my dreams, I killed people."

"Around what time would you wake up?"

"Always between two and three." She slaps her calf. "Tried all sorts of remedies. And then I turned myself over to a center for holistic therapy."

"How did it go there?"

"Well… they had a hundred different practitioners—herbalists, aroma-therapists, Pilates experts, psycho-healers… I was sent to one for digestion, to another for sleep, and then to a third for my emotional issues."

"Why to so many therapists?"

"They practice holistic medicine there. So they wanted to treat the whole of me—that is, all my problems together."

She bends forward and digs into her handbag. Scribbled notes, a hair brush, and a frayed leather key-ring fall onto the floor.

"How long did you work with —"

She plunks a pouch on my desk and shrieks its zipper open.

"See the load of herbal remedies I carry these days?" She lines three bottles. "These are for digestion." She holds up two others. "These, for my skin." Five more clink out. "And the rest, for my insomnia."

"I hope they help your emotions too."

"Are you kidding?" She glares around and fixes her gaze upon me. "You don't believe me, I know." She zips the pouch and pushes it away. "I haven't shown you all."

59

The ensemble of Karen's signs, physical and psychological, represents a disorder of her bile-energy at the root. This disorder manifested on her body and mind together. Usually, the holistic methods consider such problems at their root, and do not treat their external signs piece by piece. Unfortunately, for Karen, that was not the case.

The energetic disorders have numerous forms, each manifesting simultaneously on body and mind. Below, I show the three most common forms, in a simplified manner, with the frequencies of their physical and psychological signs occurring together under stress:

- 90% of those who suffer from acidity, poor digestion of fat, and skin allergies, also suffer from excessive anger, bitterness, cynicism, and hostile authority,

- 80% of those who suffer from frequent cold, urinary problems, and reproductive disorders, also suffer from melancholy, poor willpower, and jealousy,

- 60% of those who suffer from dry skin, accelerated intestinal transit, and rapid diction, also suffer from nervousness, fear, and loss of memory.

These energetic disorders do not remain static. They evolve, along with their physical and psychological signs. Fixing them, piece by piece, only aggravates the problem at the root; further complications occur on body and mind.

Approximately two-thirds of the people I asked had been through such piecemeal holistic therapies, for a series of problems with a common source. The essential oils, herbs, and other natural remedies, even if they are made of organic substances, are not innocuous; in excess, they leave their side effects on our organism.

Let's return to Karen:

"Their remedies worked for a month." She shifts in her seat. "Then, I started having terrible headaches. And, burning in the eyes. I saw an ophthalmologist, but there was nothing wrong with my vision."

"When you had headaches, where would they hurt?"

"Here." She presses her temples. "Then the pain would radiate to the back of my head."

"How were your pre-menstrual symptoms?"

"Oh, they became horrible. The pain would stab inside my abdomen. And dark clots came out with the menstrual blood."

"These headaches, did they peak around mid-day?"

"Yes, they did." She lines three bottles on my desk. "Two here, are for headaches. And the other one, for my PMS."

"Did you have constipation?"

"Sure. I got psyllium husk for that."

What is an 'energetic disorder'?

Sixteen meridians traverse our body, through organs such as liver, spleen, intestines, genitals, heart, and lungs. Our biodynamic energy runs through these meridians. To understand this concept better, let's use an analogy.

Imagine a meridian as a water-pipe; and, the biodynamic energy flowing through the meridian, as the water flowing through that pipe. To ensure proper water supply to a community, the pipe needs to be in good shape, and the water needs to be in good quality. If either of them deviates, the community suffers from an 'aquatic disorder'.

Similarly, to ensure proper energy supply to our organs, the meridians need to be in good shape, and the energy needs to be in good quality. If either of them deviates, the organs suffer from an 'energetic disorder'.

For example, the meridian that carries energy through the liver may deform, or the energy itself may degrade. In either case, energetic disorder of the liver occurs. Physical and psychological symptoms manifest together, such as poor digestion of fat, high cholesterol and toxicity in blood, increased light sensitivity, headaches, irritability, and bitterness.

Why do energetic disorders manifest on body and mind simultaneously?
Any disorder inside us always manifests on our body and mind together — a careful observation will show us that.

For example, when we come down with a cold, our enthusiasm falls too. Or, when our digestion falters, our temper rots too. Or, when something grates our body, something scrapes our mind too.

Our body and mind always move together.

The ancient medicines have established a stronger correlation between body and mind. A specific physical disorder is always accompanied by a specific psychological disorder. This happens because each vital organ has a two-fold energetic function: physical and psychological.

Take the liver, for example. Modern physiology says that liver's secretion, bile, emulsifies fat, as well as eliminates cholesterol and toxins. Ayurveda, the ancient medicine from India, recognizes these digestive and eliminative functions of the bile, but also asserts that bile assimilates light through the eyes, and manages anger. Ancient Chinese medicine too asserts these additional functions of the liver.

A simple observation will confirm these facts. Liver metabolizes alcohol; hence, excess drinking strains the cells of the liver. If we drink heavily one evening, the next day our eyes don't stand light well, and the slightest conflict explodes our temper.

Even Hippocrates, the father of allopathic medicine, and Hildegard Von Bingen, the mother of natural medicine, and Samuel Hahnemann, the founder of Homeopathic Medicine, confirm these links between body and mind.

What causes energetic disorders?

Both physical and psychological injuries can deform a meridian, or degrade its energy within; an energetic disorder develops from there.

For Karen, her repressed anger, a psychological factor, degraded energy inside her liver meridian; the energetic disorder of the bile revealed itself on her body and mind. A physical injury to the liver, caused by over-consumption of fat or alcohol, or by prolonged exposure to the sun, can also cause similar disorders of the bile.

Why do energetic disorders evolve over time?

The meridians within us interconnect, but, almost always, the energy inside one of them disrupts at first, causing the primary energetic disorder. This imbalance then spreads into the other meridians, causing secondary energetic disorders.

For example, Karen's primary disorder, originated from the perturbed energy inside her liver meridian. Later, this disorder spread into her reproductive meridian, and aggravated her pre-menstrual symptoms.

Are these energetic disorders diseases?

They are not, in the sense of modern medicine.

But they are precursors to diseases. If we adopt preventive measures at this stage, we avoid diseases.

Exercise 7: Discover the connections between your body and mind

You may not have experienced energetic disorders yet, but stress always pushes your biodynamic force to its limit. There, specific signs always occur on your body and mind concurrently, depending on your constitution.

To understand this concurrence, note:

> -At the beginning of stress, the physical and psychological signs that occur together,
>
> -As the stress increases, how these signs evolve.

Save this worksheet. We'll use this information in Part III, to determine your constitutional makeup.

7: Peripheral solutions ignore connection between quality and frailty

In this chapter, we'll see the third reason for failure of peripheral methods — they ignore the connection between our quality and frailty.

Let's step back and understand this connection intuitively.

Among your close relations, choose a tenacious person. You must have noticed that this person, who resists changes more fervently than others, also remains far more steadfast than the rest, when life charges you with its challenges.

Stubbornness and tenacity reside within her, side by side.

They are the two masks of her same intrinsic force, one that is ingrained in her being and doing. When insignificant matters perturb her daily habits, this force shows up as stubbornness; but, when hefty challenges arrive, the same force shows up as tenacity.

You take her, in her ensemble.

Kelly, an occupational psychologist, says:

"Strength and weakness are the two faces of the same individual."

"Can you give me an example?"

"I work a lot with artists. For these creative people, their imagination, which serves them in their work, also turns upon them in difficult times."

"You mean, when they're in distress, they imagine the worst possibilities?"

"Right. But, if they want, they can also imagine the best routes out of their plights."

"So, their imagination serves them the way they choose to use it."

"Not just them." She clears her throat. "The same holds true for people like me too, who earn their living analyzing others."

"How?"

"When I have difficulties, I could easily lose myself, analyzing all the details that jump before my eyes. Then, someone has to pinch me and say, 'See the forest first, as a whole from above, before you go down, and check the trees individually.'"

"The same analytical skill also tells you, rather quickly, which trees to chop, and which ones to keep."

"Exactly." She beams. "And to see, what link exists among those that survived."

Ancient Asian medicines affirm that *all* our qualities and frailties arise from our biodynamic force. In accordance with self, this force manifests as quality; in discordance, as frailty. Your biodynamic force is unique, with its own high and low; thus, your quality and frailty are unique too, and they always go in pair, but the peripheral methods ignore this link.

Moreover, most peripheral methods start off by hammering on frailty.

Case Study

Brenda takes an appointment with me to come in with her husband. They've been seeing a counselor for their troubled relationship. Six months ago, this counselor suggested separation.

One Saturday afternoon before Christmas they come in, each carrying two huge shopping bags.

"Gifts for your family?"

"No, for us." She takes off her fur overcoat, revealing a thick woolen jumper underneath. The air outside is chilly, but not cold enough for such layers of clothing.

"For her, mostly." Her husband snorts. "Three more pairs of shoes, and another coat."

"Brrr. It's cold in here." She closes the buttons of her sweater. "Can you please turn up the heater?"

Pouches hang under her eyes. The back of her hands look puffy. She emits a deep sigh, and sinks into the armchair. Her husband rolls his eyes.

"I started seeing the counselor first, hmm… I mean, before we started our sessions together." She hugs her arms tightly around the chest. "I had to do something about my jealousy."

"We've been together for eight years." Her husband shakes his head. "I've never seen her jealous like this before."

"What do you think changed?" I ask.

"I don't know." Her husband sits on the treatment table. "We moved here from abroad. That's where we met."

"We didn't just change place." Her face twitches. "I changed my job too, and it's horrible."

I turn toward her. "You have a lot of pressure at work?"

"Yes, there is a lot to learn for sure. On top of that, there is the pressure to perfect my French,"—her head turns toward her husband—"with my colleagues. We speak English at home."

He avoids her eyes. "I come from a provincial town. We haven't made a lot of friends here."

"And I don't know anyone outside work." Her mouth twists.

I lean back. "How do you get along with your colleagues?"

"Fine." But, her eyes narrow. "Well… let's say everything was fine, until they asked me to join a speed-dating group."

Her husband's eyebrows rise and fall.

I lean forward. "Why would they ask you to do that?"

"They want me to be more social." Her teeth grind. "They say I'm too stuck with my husband."

Her husband sways his index. "Brenda is really independent. But, for some reason,"—his jaws clench—"she can't stand my speaking to other women."

"I'm afraid, Marc!" Her eyes bulge. "I feel so insecure here. I'm sure my jealousy is coming out of that."

"What did the counselor say?"

"He thinks my jealousy has always been there. He even found reasons for it in my childhood."

"Bullshit!" Marc slaps his thigh. "I don't believe that crap. Brenda has been rock solid when we lived abroad."

69

"Thanks." Her head dips.

"Why did your counselor ask you to separate?"

"Because… he too thinks I cling to Marc." Her eyes lower. "And that's deadly for both of us."

"Don't exaggerate." Marc blows. "There has been no death, no injury."

"Looks like…" I turn from one to the other. "Neither of you truly believe that the separation would be the right thing to do."

He prunes his lips. "She doesn't cling to me as much as she thinks."

"It's not me who thinks that!" She uncrosses her arms. "Marc is right—I don't, probably." She looks away. "I could always go back to my country, start a new life, but…" Her forehead furrows.

Her husband turns toward her; she nods.

"We've stood tougher times together." She moves to the edge of her seat. "This time, I'm going to stop these ridiculous pangs of jealousy." She laughs, and then stares at her palms.

"Brenda." I roll my chair toward her. "I think you've already found a strategy."

"You think?" Her back straightens. "I hope you're right. In any case, I'll stop analyzing my jealousy. And stop talking to the colleagues about our private life."

Marc's lips part. But then he wipes his face, takes his wallet out, and shuffles the papers inside.

"Now I'll stop worrying, and start acting." She opens two buttons of her sweater. "But I feel stuck. I'm imprisoned with so much stuff around me."

"Yes, that's the other thing." Marc stands up. "She has accumulated so much stuff since we came here. She never throws anything. And she keeps buying more."

"They give me something to hold on to, Marc." She shoves her hands into the pockets of her sweater. "I don't like changing partner every two months, like my colleagues."

"Then your colleagues must admire your marital stability." I say.

"No." Her face twitches. "They think I don't have the spirit for adventure. Nor any courage."

"Do you, yourself, admire your stability?"

"Yes, I do." She slides her hands out of the pockets. "I think it's rare these days." Her chin juts toward me. "I believe, those who change partners so often, do so more out of fear than courage. More out of weakness than strength."

"What truly matters is what *you* think about yourself."

She inhales deeply and looks at her husband's face; he points his thumb up.

"Now, allow me to ask something." I roll back my chair. "These days, are you sleeping more than usual?"

"Yes, a lot." She bites her lip. "Still, it never feels like I've slept enough."

"Has your weight changed?"

71

"Yes." She clutches the fabric of her sweater. "I've put on some weight."

"Any other changes?"

"Everything feels so heavy, so sluggish. But…" Her eyes narrow. "What does weight have to do with jealousy? And, sleep?"

Later, we'll see the link among excess sleep, weight, and the rest of her issues. For now, let's focus only on the connection between her stability and jealousy.

In accordance with self, her biodynamic force revealed itself as 'stability'; but, in discordance, the same force turned into 'jealousy'. Their counselor didn't see this connection between her quality and frailty. He pounded on her jealousy alone.

As a result, he failed to reach her intimate conviction about separation.

How does discordance turn quality into frailty?
Internal accordance determines the state of our terrain.

Through this terrain, our meridians pass, and our biodynamic force flows through them. In discordance with self, the terrain deforms, which distorts the meridians, and their flow. The biodynamic force, itself, degrades under discordance.

Our quality then turns into frailty.

Does this happen only for psychological discordance?
Not always.

Internal discordance can have physical origins too. And they will still turn our quality into frailty.

For example, if bile dominates your constitution, you have a stronger digestion than others. But, the sour foods give you acidity, faster than they give others.

Say swimming suits you better, but you force yourself to run. If you're a bile-type, you have tougher muscles than others. But, the forced runs give you tendonitis, faster than they give others.

Our quality and frailty always go in pairs. The most common pairs are the following:

-98% of those who're gifted with rapid execution and creativity during periods of accordance, show nervousness and fear in discordance,

-92% of those gifted with soft authority and excellent analytics during periods of accordance, show aggression and cynicism in discordance,

-63% of those gifted with stability and attention to details during periods of accordance, show jealousy and tendency for accumulation in discordance.

Why should we be aware of this link between quality and frailty?
For prevention, at first.

In discordance with self, a creative person becomes fearful; an authoritative person, aggressive; a stable person, jealous. This awareness prevents fear, aggression, and jealousy from going out of our hands, if discordance does occur.

This knowledge has a corrective value too. By observing the manifestation of our frailty, we know when discordance has occurred within us. We realign accordance with our self, and our fear turns into creativity; our aggression, into healthy authority; and our jealousy, into stability.

We convert our frailty back into quality again.

Exercise 8: Discover the links between your quality and frailty

List what *you* perceive as your qualities, in accordance with your self; and your frailties, in discordance. Observe yourself in multiple situations.

Then, ask people in your immediate surrounding: what they perceive as your distinguishing quality, when they see you poised; and what they perceive as your remarkable frailty, when they see you perturbed. This poise or lack of it has nothing to do with the stress you're under, but has to do with whether the situation pushes you toward accordance or discordance with self.

While doing this exercise, a third of my clients discover the following about themselves: what they consider frailty is nothing but a hidden quality that protects them under discordance.

How?

Frailty protects our deformed terrain from further deterioration, by limiting its activities—the same way pain protects an injured joint from further damage, by limiting its movements.

Now see if you discover the same about yourself.

8: Our original solution fits our unique needs and adapts to our evolution

We've seen how peripheral solutions, by operating on external benchmarks, by fixing problems patch by patch, and by ignoring the connections between our quality and frailty, fail to reach our inner self.

Our original solution originates from within us.

We may have to work with one or several practitioners, but we personalize their methods and obtain our original solution, which fulfils our unique needs, as well as fits our unique course of evolution. This requires us to identify our needs at each stage of evolution—that is, what we have to do to align ourselves with our personal benchmarks.

Thus, we start our journey by looking inside us, to establish those personal benchmarks.

Establishing them also allows us to view ourselves from above.

We don't see us as an assembly of isolated parts; rather, we see how different parts of our body and mind connect together, move together. We don't have to be a doctor or a therapist to notice the following: what we eat affects not only our digestion, but also our sleep; and what we think affects not only our sleep, but also our digestion.

Once we've established our personal benchmarks, we adjust the different components of our lifestyle, either with a practitioner or by ourselves. We don't fix our problems piece by piece; rather, knowing that *all* our issues, physiological and psychological, have a common root, we seek a solution for that root problem.

Accordance with self sets in us, naturally.

This analysis makes us aware of our qualities. We prevent our frailties, even transform them into qualities; our repertoire of strengths enlarges. Accordance with self eliminates our inner conflicts; our internal efficiency improves. Our overall performance increases as a result; we distinguish ourselves from the rest.

This distinction reinforces our self-esteem. Life sparkles within us, and our confidence takes a leap.

In course of evolution, this heightened confidence makes further adjustments to our original solution easier. Robust to uncertainties, we push ahead steadfast, and keep evolving, without ever losing accordance again.

In chapter 4, we saw how Beatrice personalized her group methods, in order to construct her original solution. In individual sessions, where the problems are usually more complex, the practitioners have to guide their clients more, in devising their solutions. Nevertheless, your original solution still has to originate from within you.

Let's see how Stephan, Karen, and Brenda from the last three chapters arrived at their solutions.

Stephan's original solution

Stephan accepted his natural cycle of sleep without further help from me. A new problem cropped up; he called me for an appointment.

Odor of cigarette fills my office, as he drags himself in.

"Chronic bronchitis, Monsieur Garai." He grunts. "Can you guess why?"

"Are you on medications?"

"Only this." He slaps a pack of cigarette on my desk.

His complexion is pale; his jaw muscles, stiff.

"How many per day, Stephan?"

"Five, ten, twenty… All depends on my meter of frustration."

"Why did you start—"

"Destroying myself?" He shakes his head. "Good question."

"You should go to your doctor first."

"Bye then." He stands up. "Sorry I wasted your time."

"Okay, okay. Tell me what's happening in your job."

"I've been put in the closet." Three horizontal lines crease his forehead.

"Explain please."

"My boss and I, we fought over our project." He slumps in the armchair. "Now, all I do is—pushing papers around."

"Your boss put a throttle on your steam."

"He would have fired me if he could." His lower lip protrudes. "You know how it feels, when the meat smells great in your bowl, but your leash has been tied too short."

"I do. But, you're not one who stays tied, Stephan. I'm sure you've taken the necessary steps."

78

"You bet." His back slides up. "Have pulled a few strings higher up. Results will show, most probably, but…" He sighs. "But I have no patience. So I'm smoking myself up in the meantime." His nostrils crinkle.

"Do you really enjoy smoking?"

"Enjoy?" His eyes avert. "Not really. Plus, my breath stinks."

"Are you continuing your sports?"

"Would you, if you had lungs stuffed like a turkey?" He taps his knuckles on the chest. "Sports do nothing for my pent-up energy. So I picked up these bastards." He lifts his cigarette pack.

"Frustration, pent-up energy, bastards… Come on, Stephan, what's happening?"

"I know, I know." He raises his hands above the head. "My self-esteem is at its lowest."

"For your boss, you've done what felt right." I stand up. "Now, divert your energy, away from you."

"My damn energy!" He hits his palm. "It's destroying me."

"The same energy reconstructed you, only a couple of months ago."

"You're right." He looks up. "It's not the fault of my energy." He rubs his nails. "It's my fault indeed. I just don't have the patience."

"It's okay to have faults. Now, think of a means to divert your energy."

"Doing sports isn't enough?"

"Sports will help you, but not divert that kind of energy. You need a passion that absorbs you, completely."

"Like home repair and that kind of stuff?"

"A passion that brings you closer to your heart."

He scratches his chin. "I'll have to think."

Eight weeks later, Stephan returns.

"I picked up music again." He takes out a metal flute from his attaché case, and rolls it over my desk. "Lost touch with it for decades, but the return was a real experience."

"Do you carry it to your work?"

"Yes, but not to charm my boss." He sniffs. "He has backed off, by the way."

"How?"

He leans back. "We both attended a workshop on conflict management. Since then, we don't clash anymore."

"I see you stopped smoking."

"That's where this worked like a magic." He clinks the flute. "I couldn't think of a real passion off the top of my head. So, one Sunday morning, I climbed into the attic and found this flute."

"How long have you had it?"

"Since twelve. Uncle gave it to me." He takes out a binder. "Found my sheets of music too." He flaps through them. "All tucked away, neatly, waiting for me." A smile lifts his cheeks. "I even found my hand-written notes from then."

"I can imagine you, Stephan, in that attic."

"Really?" His eyes sparkle. "I tried my first song right up there. And it took me to a different world." His gaze moves up. "To my world."

"When do you play?"

"At night, before the children sleep." His gaze returns to me. "I've started taking the flute to my work too. At lunch break, I play on the river shore."

"I can see why you no longer need those cigarettes."

"I hated them anyway." His nostrils flinch. "They tasted so bitter."

"How long did it take you to quit smoking?"

"Well…I read somewhere: 'One should cut smoking gradually.' But… that doesn't fit me quite right." His hand chops. "I cut it in one shot."

"How did you stop your impulsions afterward?"

"With this." He raises the flute. "Those impulsions get only the wimps, Monsieur Garai. And I'm not one."

"Bravo, Stephan!"

He clanks the flute on his head. "When the cravings came real strong, I recalled the notes I had played."

"That dispersed the cravings."

He nods. "Before, I stuck to those sheets, note by note. Now, I improvise my own."

"You redirected your energy into creation."

"May be." He pinches his chin. "Yes, that's exactly what happened."

"You threw your cigarettes?"

"Yes. For a while, they disgusted me." His face winces. "They reminded me of my sufferings. I even hated those who smoked near me."

"Then, that repulsion must have made you suffer too."

He startles. "You're right! Repulsion hurts as much as addiction." He slides his fingers along the flute. "Today, I'm indifferent to cigarettes. They neither tempt me nor disgust me."

"You became more robust by focusing on your core."

"I couldn't have done that without my flute."

Among my clients, 96% of those who had quit their addictions confirmed the following.

They were dependent on food, alcohol, cigarettes, narcotics, or drugs, because either they didn't see their evolutions, or they felt stuck in situations that were not in accordance with them.

Stagnation generates boredom.

Boredom oppresses our nervous system, and depresses the neurotransmitters that carry neural electricity to the various parts of our organism. We feel low; at our limits, desperate. The addictives boost these neurotransmitters; we feel high, but only temporarily.

In fact, we climb out of the frying pan, to fall into the fire.

Once the effects of the addictives subside, we sink even lower in our misery. To come up, we need a stronger addictive, in a larger quantity. The vicious cycle continues, until our neurons lose their sensibilities altogether. Then we feel no pain, no pleasure.

We become stoned—the 'unanimated souls'.

All my clients who gave up addictions successfully took the following steps:

    - They eliminated *all* stagnations from their personal and professional lives,

    - They transformed their energy, from destructive into constructive, by a true passion,

    - And they revived their nervous system through yoga, Tai Chi, Pilates, and sports.

Let's return to Stephan.

    "What else did you notice since you quit smoking?"

    "See my skin?" He rolls up his sleeve. "When I smoked, it was all dry, flaky like a snake." He touches his forearm. "I quit smoking, and my skin recovered its health in three weeks."

    "Did you use any special creams, or oils?"

    "No. Happened all by itself." His eyes gleam, but then his forehead furrows. "What a pity!"

    "What's wrong now?"

    "I killed my skin smoking those bastards." He sighs, shaking his head. "What a stupid idea it was!"

    "A snake never worries about its skin."

    "Why?"

    "It knows the skin will grow back again."

How does smoking destroy the skin?

Bronchitis, gruff voice, and low stamina are common consequences of smoking—we all know that. The ancient Asian medicines, however, attribute further energetic consequences to the invasion of the lung meridian:

Digested food elements enter the bloodstream and diffuse into the cells, where the fire of cellular digestion cooks them. This cellular cooking needs oxygen. The lungs extract that oxygen from air.

The cellular cooking releases the nutritive energy from these foods, which then mixes with the cosmic energy from air, and creates the vital energy. This vital energy then spreads throughout the organism via the meridians. Among them, the lung meridians distribute this energy to the skin.

Congested lungs can't extract oxygen from air effectively; food elements don't cook properly inside the cells; production of vital energy falls within the organism. Moreover, congested lung meridians can't bring enough vital energy, which is already poor in quality, to the skin.

The skin loses its luster and texture.

The damage from smoking doesn't stop at the lungs, or at the skin.

The Asian medicines couple lungs with colon. The beneficial bacteria inside the colon defend our organism against harmful beings, such as bacteria, fungi, virus, and cancerous cells. Weak lungs mean a weak colon; a weak colon means a weak immunity; and a weak immunity means vulnerability to fatal diseases.

On the psychological plane, the lung-colon pair manages melancholy, nervousness, and fear—we've seen these emotions in Stephan already, when he was smoking.

Note how Stephan constructed his original solution.

He didn't take one remedy for bronchitis, another for skin, and a third for nervousness. He linked *all* his issues, physical and mental, to the root of the problem: smoking. He quit smoking.

He also saw that his repressed energy pushed him toward smoking. While he sorted out his professional conflicts, he released that energy by playing flute. Along the course of his evolution, he redirected this energy into improvising songs.

His energy changed label, from 'destructive' to 'constructive'.

***

Karen's original solution

Karen returned to that centre for holistic medicine, and chose only one therapist.

This person estimated that her hyperactive liver and gall bladder meridians lay at the root of all her troubles, and administered the appropriate therapy to correct her hyperactivity.

Karen, herself, didn't sit idle:

"Somehow, I felt all my symptoms were connected with anger."

"What made you see this connection?"

"I started taking notes." She takes out a writing pad. "I saw, whenever I repressed anger, I woke up with nightmares. The morning after, my head pounded, and I had no appetite." She dents her upper abdomen. "The dinner from the night before sat here."

"Did your food habit change?"

"Oh, yes." She flurries through the pages and folds one. "I ate too many sweets, too much creamy stuff." Her jaws clench. "Anger made me slave to those junks."

"Do you still —"

"No, I cut them."

"How?"

"Just like that." Her hand slices. "I didn't need someone to whisper wisdom in my ears."

What links anger to craving for sweets?
Anger inflames us.

Inflammation damages our terrain, our nerves and vessels. To prevent this damage, our natural mechanism of auto-correction pushes us toward sweets.

A little bit of sweet balances our terrain; our craving disappears.

But, if we repress anger, our organism can't distinguish between healthy and perverted desires for sweets; so, we consume too much. Over-consumption increases our craving further, and instills a vicious cycle; phlegm develops within us.

Phlegm congests our organs, impedes the passage of nutrients and excrements; toxins accumulate everywhere.

Let's return to Karen:

"I stopped drinking alcohol too."

"Why did you consume alcohol?"

"It soothed my anger, made me forget my sufferings." Her forehead crinkles. "A glass of wine helps the heart, right?"

"You think?"

"Not really." She sniffles. "In moments of frustration, alcohol did release my tension." Her eyes lower. "But, next morning, I woke up angrier. So, in the evening, I drank even more. And things went worse from there."

"Did you really enjoy drinking?"

"No. It gave me nausea."

"So what did you replace it with?"

"Swimming and Pilates."

In anger, does alcohol really help our heart?
Let's think together.

Anger constricts blood vessels; our blood pressure rises. To pump blood against this elevated pressure, our heart slogs and drags. What changes, when we drink alcohol?

Molecules of alcohol reach our hypothalamus and medulla oblongata, stimulate the centers for vasomotor control, and dilate our blood vessels. The blood pressure falls, the heart pumps easier; we relax.

Next day, when the alcohol molecules subside, our blood vessels constrict again, but a little more than before; so, our heart has to work harder. To dilate our vessels, we need a larger quantity of alcohol, which increases our consumption. The day after, our vessels constrict even more, and…

From there on, the story goes sorry for our heart.

Alcohol doesn't help our liver either.

The molecules of alcohol decompose inside the cells of our liver. Each time our consumption increases, our liver has to work harder. The cells of our liver tire, and degenerate. Weak liver produces weak bile; our digestion suffers.

Ancient Asian medicines also say that the degeneration of liver increases our light sensitivity, headaches, constipation, menstrual disorders, problems of skin and joints, as well as our anger, cynicism, and bitterness.

To eliminate anger, or any other strong emotions, we can spare these damages to our heart and liver.

In part I, we saw how observing strong emotions, instead of denying them, reduces their intensity. Yoga, especially its breathing protocols, Pilates, and Tai-Chi stimulate the vasomotor control centers, and dilate our blood vessels naturally. These exercises also slow our respiration and heart-beats; the emotions lose their intensity.

Running, swimming, bicycling, and any aerobic sport at a brisk pace also evacuate repressed emotions, free us from their overpowering grip.

We can then think cerebrally, deal with the problem at its source.

Let's see how Karen did:

"My situation was not tenable." She rubs her palm on the trouser. "So, I decided to switch job."

"Have you, already?"

"Not yet." Her gaze shifts. "For now, I've accepted to look for a job. That has taught me a lesson."

"How?"

"I discovered something eye-opening about my anger." She prunes her lips. "It started with me."

"Why were you angry with yourself?"

"I was angry because —" her eyes fog "—I let myself suffer in that deadlock. That made me harsh toward myself. I left no margin for errors." Her gaze traces the lower perimeter of the wall. "And, of course—" she swallows "—I made even more errors."

I turn toward her.

"Then I was angrier." She crumples a sheet of paper. "Not only for those errors, but also for the time I lost fixing them." She bites her lower lip.

I lean forward.

"Whoever came my way, became a victim of that anger, including my boss…uh-huh…my former colleague."

"Since you decided to change job, has your relation with this person evolved?"

"Before, I would keep talking to her, inside my head. Words, full of rage, non-stop. Dream vengeance against —"

"Karen, let's step out of that trap. Has your attitude toward her changed?"

"Changed? Ah." Her hand slides down her thigh. "Yes, gentler."

"Why?"

"I guess, because…" Her index circles her knee cap. "I became a lot gentler toward me. I let myself pull out of that suffering."

"This happened when you decided to change job?"

"Yes. The noose of anger loosened immediately. Those monologues of rage, those dreams of vengeance disappeared. Can you believe? I even recognized her strengths!"

"Great, Karen!"

"When you feel stuck with someone, you don't see her qualities. You only see her defects." She nods. "But, when you know you're leaving, you start seeing her good sides."

"Do you still want to quit your job?"

"Yes I do." She straightens her lapels. "Everyone doesn't have to, but, for me, yes. And I don't regret that. The experience has taught me how to handle my emotions better."

"And, how to admire the qualities of your opponents."

"She's a talented person, I agree. But, I could never accept her as my boss." She leans back. "What I did works the best for me."

***

Brenda's original solution

Brenda didn't separate from her husband; instead, she separated from her jealousy:

"I started by getting rid of my things,"—she flings her hand—"all those useless stuff I had accumulated over the years."

"What made you take that route?"

"You made me think there is a link between putting on weight and stocking up materials. So, I looked at my charts. My weight went up just around the times I bought more stuff." Her thumb traces the crease of her elbow. "It took me a while to believe that, but the link was clearly there."

"So you started throwing things away."

"I needed to act, not analyze anymore. So I said: 'Just see how your jealousy increased, as you gathered more things. Now, what would happen to your jealousy, if you threw those things?'"

"You threw your jealousy with them."

"No! I couldn't throw those things at the beginning." Her eyes glisten. "But, my husband found a great strategy."

I lean forward.

"He said: 'Let's wrap everything you haven't used in six months, and put them in boxes. We'll take them to the cellar.' So, we packed a dozen boxes, and took them down. There, he said, 'If you don't open those for a year, we'll dump them in the garbage truck.'"

"The strategy worked?"

"Amazingly well." Her mouth opens large. "More than sixteen thousands Euros, Monsieur Garai. Can you believe? I took the boxes to the local church, though."

"Did you regret losing money?"

She sways her index. "I would have, if I didn't see the lesson from it." Her forehead furrows. "Those things hung around my ankles like prisoner's weights."

"Now you're free again."

She nods. "Ready to move, lean and clean."

"Have you been exercising?"

"I've picked up running since then, and yoga." She taps her knuckles on the desk. "Shoulder stand sheds weight, right?"

"True."

"I've lost weight steadily, one to two kilos a month. I could have lost more, with those crazy diets, but…"

"They don't go with you."

"Right! Their approach is so sadist."

"Why?"

"Well…first you starve yourself to death. Then, you crave like you're in famine." Her face twitches. "Of course you lose weight, but with so much resentment." She clacks her heel. "Then, one day, you crush your diet, eat like mad, and inflate like a balloon."

"You end up with more weight than you had before."

"Yes." She shivers.

"Why do you think that happens?"

"Your body anticipates the next famine and stocks up."

"What did you do to lose weight?"

"Ate less at each meal, did sports regularly." She lifts her eyes. "And the shoulder-stand, twice per day."

"What else did you notice?"

"My mood lifted." Her chest thrusts forward. "True, other factors improved around me too, but…" She smacks her lips. "I could see what the shoulder-stand did for my mood."

"Really?"

She leans forward. "When my courage failed, I would drop everything, and hold the posture for five minutes. Then, when I came down, my mood went up! I mean, you can really feel that lift."

"What did you feel precisely?"

"For example, every time I felt depressed, a lump would block me here." She places her palm under the throat. "When I went into shoulder-stand, warmth flew to that spot, and melted the lump away."

"How long did the relief last?"

"Oh, many hours. Then I started doing the posture more often, and my mood fell even less."

"You became more robust."

"Monsieur Garai, I thought you would ask me: 'Brenda, what organ is there, under your throat?'"

"Sorry, Brenda. What organ is there under your throat?"

"Thymus gland." She beams.

"Close. What does thymus gland do?"

"Defends our organism." Her eyes narrow.

"What other gland benefits from the shoulder-stand?"

"Ah, the thyroid." She inhales. "It's the thyroid that benefits the most from shoulder stand."

"What does thyroid do?"

"Regulates our metabolism."

"That's all?"

"I looked up the Sanskrit word for shoulder-stand: 'Sarvangasana'. It consists of three separate words: 'Sarva' meaning all, 'Anga' meaning limb, and 'Asana' meaning posture."

"So, what did you conclude?"

"This *one* posture takes care of all our organs."

"How do you think—"

"It does all that by taking care of our thyroid."

Let's step aside and see how shoulder-stand acts upon our thyroid:

In this posture, the gravity rushes blood to our throat. This extra blood would have reached our brain via the carotid arteries, but the lock of the chin against the sternum compresses those arteries. The extra blood flow is deviated, via the thyroid arteries, to our thyroid; its cells bathe in the nutritive elements of our blood.

The posture also opens the thyroid vein, thus drains its congestions and toxins.

Overall, the cells of our thyroid revitalize. Their hormone, thyroxin, improves in quality. Thyroxin determines our basic metabolic rate, thus our weight, and the robustness of our mood.

The posture also drains congestion from our pelvic cavity. This improves the health of our reproductive glands, and their secretions. The hormones from these glands, and those from the thyroid, reinforce each other.

Our metabolism improves further, and our mood becomes more robust.

If we do a sedentary profession, shoulder-stand alone does not suffice to regulate our metabolism and mood. We need to do a minimum of thirty minutes of cardiovascular activity, at 130% to 150% of our resting pulse rate.

Many do fast walk to their work.

Such cardiovascular activities stimulate our heart and lungs. The tissues of our muscles and organs pick up more blood and oxygen; our basic metabolic rate rises. Moreover, these activities release more endorphins in our blood. These endorphins kill pain and elevate our mood.

The well-being that results from these natural thyroxin and endorphins lasts for many hours after those activities cease. And, when we do them with the awareness of evolution, our self-esteem heightens.

Let's see how that helped Brenda.

"The image I have of myself today is radically different." She tucks her chin in. "I don't think all that came from doing sports and yoga only. Nor from throwing things blindly."

"So, you did analyze yourself a bit?"

"That's my vice, Monsieur Garai." She sighs. "Getting lost in details."

"But, when attention to details *is* required, your vice becomes your virtue."

"Right." Her index traces the crest of her chin. "I didn't believe that before, but I do now."

"What did your analysis conclude?"

"Going materially lean made me psychologically lean too." Her eyes glitter. "Brought me closer to who I am really."

Excess materials make us stagnate. When we push material excess away, we clear our path for evolution. In a study, I pushed a group of clients, who admitted material excess, to do the following:

- Identify their unique talents at work,

- With their managers, reorganize their roles around those talents,

- And then enhance those talents through specific trainings. Among them, only 73% decided to try.

Among those who tried, 96% distinguished themselves at work. And, they eliminated their material excess, within four and a half months on average.

They didn't shed their material excess alone. Emotionally, they became a lot leaner too. And, they shed their excess weight, 68% on average.

More stagnated we feel, heavier we are; freer we feel, leaner we become.

Exercise 9: Revise your original solution

If you have come up to here, you already have a panoramic view of yourself:

- Of your personal benchmarks;
- Of the physical and psychological signs of your unwell-being, if any;
- And of the connection between your quality and frailty.

You also have a blueprint of your original solution—detailed to cover all possibilities, but maybe a bit cumbersome.

Don't worry. Most of my clients present the same abundance of details at this stage. From here, you've to leave that comfortable abundance, and go for a solution more precise. You *can* now.

Because, at this stage you know, intuitively, what's essential for you.

The ascension to your original solution becomes steeper from here. To climb further, you need confidence to leave all the non-essentials behind. But, you *have* acquired this confidence, on the path you've already traversed. From now on, the vision of the solution at the summit will push you, steadfast, through the challenges ahead.

Knowing what's essential, for you, is not a conscious process entirely. Your heart and your instincts guide you in that search.

For example: Stephan knew he had to redirect his energy; Karen knew she had to change job; Brenda knew she had to respect her stability. The process is far from being purely psychological either. Your senses work, hand-in-hand, with your unconscious, and guide you. Stephan knew cigarettes didn't go with his taste; Karen knew she didn't appreciate alcohol; Brenda knew material excess blocked her path.

Many balk at this stage, unable to trust their instincts and senses—faculties we no longer use as much. Nevertheless, they continue to exist in us. If you step back and look at your original solution, you'll discover you've used them already. Going forward, you can only do better.

Let's start with a big clean-up.

Take a closer look at your original solution. From a standpoint of courage and confidence, take the weeds out, and focus on the essential only—what's truly important to *you*. Then, step back, and look at the ensemble.

Do these essentials connect somehow?
Yes. Scrutinize those connections closer.

Any parts still don't feel essential?

Take them out. Step back again, and look at the leaner version as a whole.

Do a few peaks look disconnected from the rest, but you can't take them out?

Don't worry. As you climb higher, you'll see the landscape below that connects those peaks.

In part III, we'll see two examples of original solutions, complete and concrete.

Exercise 10: Strengthen your inner voice

We've almost reached the end of the part II. Before we move on, let's try the following exercise.

We all quote famous people, but we rarely live by those quotes. This shows: our hearts are not in accordance with them. Can we write quotes that will convince us truly—quotes we can live up to? Let's find out.

- Take a fresh sheet of paper. At the bottom, write the first quote of a famous person that crosses your mind, and leave the sheet aside for the day.

- By the end of the day, a quote of your own would surface within you. Most of my clients say this usually happens just before they fall asleep. Write this quote, at the *top* of the same sheet.

- Next day, live by this quote of yours.

You've just given yourself, and your interior voice, a place in this world. Do this once per week, and, in a year, you'll have fifty-two quotes of your own to live by.

Our life is too short to live by the quotes of others. The only way to feel you have lived *your* life is to live by your own quotes, which you believe firmly; everything else is redundant.

Your own quotes arise from your heart alone—from those intimate experiences you've lived through, and assimilated into your being. Your heart is always speaking to you, but you hear its voice only after you've given yourself a firm place in this world. From then on, your inner voice rises above all, and the external noises fade away within you.

You live, and work, in true inner silence.

Continue this exercise until you've replaced *all* quotes of others, by the quotes of your own. As you go on, note how your thoughts, perceptions, and actions evolve.

Part III

We can build our original solution
easily, from inside out

9: By knowing when to correct

Until now, we've seen only a part of how to construct original solutions. We've assumed people already had the key to their self—that is, the fundamental belief that sits deep within them, and governs all their actions. This belief can go buried under stress.

In this part, we'll see how to recover that fundamental belief, achieve accordance with self, and fine-tune our original solution. There is, however, one more step before that.

Others can exaggerate our unwell-being. In chapter 5, Stephan's wife did, with his insomnia. And, the corrective measures ruined his natural efficiency, dampened his enthusiasm for life.

About 16% of my clients overcorrect. This taxes their organism, often severely:

Julia, 32 years old, stewardess, takes laxatives for her chronic constipation.

"Since I started those long haul flights, I don't go to the toilet regularly." Her forehead furrows. "Sometimes, two days in a row."

"How regular was your intestinal transit before?"

"I went every other day."

"What else have you noticed?"

"My breath." Her nose crinkles. "It bothers my husband too."

"How long have you been taking laxatives?"

"Eighteen months. Every day." She sighs. "I had my colon cleansed last week."

"How did that go?"

"They said it looks like a plastic tube now." She shakes her head. "And, that's not the whole story."

She bites her lip. "Those laxatives deregulated my menstruation too. So, I took contraceptive pills."

"To regulate your cycles?"

"I was told they work."

"Did they?"

"They gave me fluid retention." Her lip curls. "So, I took diuretics." She turns her face aside. "Those inflamed my kidneys."

Constipation, beyond three to four days at a time, generates dangerous toxins, by putrefying the fecal matters within the colon. These toxins then seep into our blood, circulate throughout the body, and deposit on the organs, joints, and nerves; our organism degenerates slowly.

We must seek expert advice if constipation becomes severe and chronic.

Julia's constipation was not that abnormal. She overcorrected by taking laxatives, and this caused her a series of problems, far more serious. We want to avoid such overcorrection.

That's why our first step is: *knowing when to correct.*

Our body has a mechanism of auto-correction

A healthy organism regulates itself:

Example 1

Let's say your boss announces that you have a presentation before the Board of Directors after lunch. The announcement punches your stomach, but you stand up to the event.

Your organism prepares for the challenge; all your strengths come into play, with their best. Your brain sends a series of signals to the adrenals, and they spurt adrenaline into your blood. Your vigilance increases, your courage boosts, your blood sugar rises—all this, to give you more energy for the action.

But, your organism pays a price. The same adrenaline constricts your blood vessels, raises your blood pressure. Your digestive glands cut their flow of enzymes; you don't digest your lunch well.

After the presentation, your stress falls.

Your brain sends a new series of signals that stop the adrenaline. Your blood pressure falls to its usual level; your vigilance becomes normal; you can calm down and relax. Your digestive juices flow normally again; you digest your dinner better.

Your organism returns to its 'zero point'—the state before announcement.

You don't need to do a thing.

Example 2

The death of someone close shocks you. Pressure builds within your head, your chest tightens, and a lump blocks your throat.

These obstructions disrupt your neural signals, change your hormones, and alter your blood chemistry. If this continues for too long, your body and mind will suffer seriously. So your organism figures it must do something to release that grip of oppression.

You cry.

While tear glands produce tear, other glands release corrective biochemical molecules in the blood. Your blood carries these molecules to the brain, to the nerve centers in your chest and throat, and to the endocrine glands. Your neural signals and hormones flow normally again; your blood restores its biochemical balance; and the pressure releases from your chest and throat.

Free from oppressions, you let go on your grief, and take charge of the situation.

Your organism returns to its 'zero point', on its own.

Example 3

Say you chomp on a chili. Your mouth burns, you breathing accelerates, and your heart pounds; you boil inside and sweat.

Instinctively, you reach for water.

Why?

Your taste buds relay the 'fire' of chili to the brain. Your organism generates heat in excess. To ventilate that heat, your lungs and heart accelerate. Your organism also pushes you to consume water, and the 'fire' extinguishes.

You return to your 'zero'.

But auto-correction fails under panic

Auto-correction is done by a system of feedback: an increase of force in one direction is balanced by a counterforce in the opposite direction.

For example, when adrenaline constricts our blood vessels, our brain sends a counteractive signal that prevents those vessels from constricting too much. As a result, although our blood pressure rises under stress, it doesn't increase so much as to explode our vessels, or fail our heart. Once stress ceases, our nervous and endocrinal systems work together, and bring the organism back to its 'zero'.

All these happen, unconsciously, as long as our organism perceives stress within a reasonable limit.

Under panic—that is, extreme stress—our balancing mechanism collapses. The counteractive forces disappear; or, worse, they reinforce each other. For example, the signals from our brain elevate our blood pressure, already high, even further. Our organism slips into a vicious cycle, and continues that way, until a total breakdown occurs.

After this, the organism can't return to its 'zero', on its own.

We can, however, prevent this breakdown, by directing our awareness inside, by trusting our auto-regulation to do the job alone. This is where the awareness exercise from chapter 2 becomes highly effective. By renouncing our grip on body and mind, we reinforce the strength of our auto-correction.

The vicious cycle breaks, and our organism returns to its 'zero'.

What is our organism's 'zero point'?
The zero of our organism is its state of 'dynamic equilibrium', balance in motion.

This state represents an ensemble of physiological indicators such as blood pressure, blood sugar, pulse rate, breathing rate, digestion, sleep, and energy; as well as psychological indicators such as perception, analysis, intuition, and emotions.

All these indicators are maintained at their optimal levels, unconsciously, without our knowing or doing anything about them.

Each organism has its unique zero. At this point, the organism operates optimally, by employing its qualities at their best, and by provoking its frailties at their least. This is the state for its best effectiveness, at maximal efficiency.

When we're operating in accordance with self, we are at this state of dynamic equilibrium. We have minimal friction within ourselves, and with those around us.

Who maintains our 'zero'?
Our nervous and endocrinal systems.

They do this job by transmitting signals to the various parts of our organism, but each does it differently:

- Our nervous system transmits information by neural impulses along our nerves. These transmissions are quick, but their effects don't last long.

- Our endocrinal system transmits information by hormones along our blood flow. These transmissions are slow, but their effects last long.

Together, our nervous and endocrinal systems communicate with the billions of cells in our body, and regulate their activities. All these happen for only one objective—to keep our organism alive, healthy, and efficient. The interdependence between these two systems becomes the most critical under stress.

To understand this, we have to know the basics of their physiology. We already know how our adrenal glands secrete adrenaline in response to stress, but the role of our nervous system in managing stress may be a bit subtler to grasp.

The part of our nervous system that manages stress has two branches: the 'sympathetic' branch that accelerates our organism, under stress; and the 'parasympathetic' branch that restores our organism, after stress. They execute these functions by secreting neurotransmitters, which carry neural signals across the nerves. But, our hormones also come into play in managing stress.

For example, the adrenaline and the neurotransmitters from the sympathetic branch accelerate our heart, but the neurotransmitters from the parasympathetic branch decelerate it.

Our heart still beats faster than usual, but not so fast as to fail.

Once stress stops, the endorphins clean our organism, and restore it to its zero point.

This does not happen, however, if panic takes over.

As soon as our organism *perceives* stress as extreme, it panics.

The balancing coordination between our nervous and endocrinal systems falls apart. The sympathetic branch speeds up further, while the parasympathetic branch slows down. At the same time, the adrenals inject more adrenaline into our blood.

These hormones and neurotransmitters reinforce each other, intensify the effects of panic. We slip into a vicious cycle, and then collapse eventually.

The zero of our organism shifts abruptly; we enter the zone of strain.

Notice the accent on the word 'perceives' four paragraphs before. The same stress is perceived as panic by some and strains their organisms, while it's perceived as normal by others and does not strain their organisms. This perception depends on where their zero point lies already.

Perception of panic depends on the position of the zero; and this position of zero depends on the perception of panic. In other words, they influence each other.

Particularly, in the zone of strain, they deteriorate each other.

Panic shifts our zero point abruptly, but prolonged stress without panic can also make this shift happen progressively.

For example, at work, when we take a simple challenge as menace, a diluted panic lingers over us, for many hours. Our heart beats slightly faster than usual; our blood pressure and blood sugar rise a little above their normal levels; our enzyme secretions and intestinal movements fall a little below normal.

In other words, our zero shifts a little bit, but for many hours.

After work, the acute stress winds down. Our heart slows; our blood sugar, blood pressure, enzyme secretions, and intestinal movements return to near normal. Our zero shifts back too, but not entirely.

It stays a little farther from where it was before.

Next day, if another diluted panic occurs, our zero point shifts a little farther.

Over the long term, the effects of these mini-panics accumulate, and shift our zero significantly.

Our organism's zero is its point of maximal efficiency. Any shift, either way, impedes us from functioning effectively.

The shift grates our body and mind perpetually, prevents us from being Zen. All frictions, however, do not mean a permanent shift of zero has occurred. Some discomforts are normal in a running organism, and they don't need corrections.

Let's see when.

The equilibrium of our organism is not static but dynamic

I was alarmed by the number of people who had sound health but complained of 'not being Zen'. Below, I've grouped what they meant really:

- 43% said they were never 'perfectly happy'
- 38% said they were never 'totally at ease'
- 19% said they were never 'absolutely calm'

When I asked them how they chose these criteria, they said this is what they've been made to believe, by others.

The word 'Zen', of Indo-European origin, entered English in 1727. Its Sanskrit root *dhya* means 'to see, to understand'; and the corresponding Greek root *sa* means 'to shine, to mark by distinction'. In being Zen, we obtain tranquility, by distinguishing ourselves through a series of actions—by seeing and understanding our relationship with the Universe, as well as by living and working in synergy with its forces.

All those verbs above are *dynamic*.

How many of those—'perfectly happy', 'totally at ease', and 'absolutely calm'—are dynamic?

Or, make an effort to understand, act, and distinguish?

How many of those ever leave their cocoons, worry about going somewhere, or do something meaningful with their lives?

Not many.

The authentic image associated with 'being Zen' is one of a machine running smoothly in balance—that is, equilibrium in motion. When we are Zen, our organism functions without jerks, and our interactions with others have no jitter.

A Zen organism is robust to pressure, and resilient to shocks. Stress can perturb it, but only temporarily. It adapts without squeaks, and returns to its zero, when stress disappears.

How does one achieve tranquility then?
A tranquil person is one who sees himself evolving, going somewhere.

A person stuck in his place, itches. Among my clients, nine out of ten who complained of depression, irritability, lack of willpower, low vitality, and poor personal hygiene attributed their conditions to feeling stagnant in life.

Not seeing their evolution, they lived and worked mechanically; their self-esteem sank. Not resolving their existential issues, they lost motivation; sloth slithered into them. Not feeling any spiritual uplift, they gave in to material excess; sloppiness seeped into their lives.

On the contrary, being Zen requires us to evolve in action. We witness our evolution from one point to another, as a result of our work. We put in our best efforts, where our competence truly belongs, and keep our eyes on the evolution. We accept that the material outcomes of our work depend *also* on the factors outside us.

Why is that important?

Unfavorable circumstances can destroy the material outcomes of our work. If we remained focused only on the material outcomes, we would have the impression of returning to where we were before. We'll not see how, as a result of our actions, we evolved from one point to the next.

Every action evolves us.

And that evolution stays with us, no matter what happens to the material outcomes of our actions. No unfavorable circumstances can ever rob us of our evolution. If we take this simple fact to our heart, we'll never feel stagnant at our place and itch.

Being Zen is to be aware of our evolution, while doing our task right.

Evolution is the sign of a free person. We are the only true witness of our own evolution. And, witnessing this appeases us profoundly. There is another benefit from remaining focused on our evolution: we don't become impatient to see only the final results of our actions, and ignore the rest of the process. We also take pleasure from the intermediate steps of our tasks, and extract learning from each one of them.

We embrace the totality of our task, gracefully.

This grace lubricates our organism; it runs without fatigue and squeaks. This grace also renews our enthusiasm for life. We no longer look ten years back—how young and vulnerable we were; instead, we look ten years ahead—how experienced and dignified we would be.

Being Zen, we don't waste our energy on matters we have no control over; we leave those to settle on their own. We concentrate our energy on the unique talents we have, where we are at our best.

This focus takes us where we're truly meant to go.

Why some disequilibrium is normal in a running organism

What is the basic requirement for movement?

Differentials.

A water pump creates differentials of pressure; the water flows. A generator creates differentials of voltage; the electricity flows.

Inside our body, the blood flows because our heart creates pressure differentials; the neural electricity flows because our brain creates voltage differentials. All flows inside our organism occur because of differentials. Our life continues because these imbalances invoke and maintain these flows inside us.

Flows generate friction, as water does inside pipes, or electricity inside wires. But, all flows do not burst pipes or burn wires. The organic flows generate friction within us for sure, but they do not damage our body or mind necessarily. A Zen person, immersed in the passion for work, and aware of his evolution, does not notice these frictions.

The flows pass through him imperceptibly.

When do these flows hurt us?

Our organism is a river of many flows.

A river flows from high to low. As long as the differential of water levels stays moderate, the flow nourishes the river bed, turns turbines smoothly, and generates electricity that feeds the villages along the river. When the differential rises too high, the flow erodes the river bed, breaks turbines, and inundates those villages.

When the differentials of blood pressure remain moderate, the blood flow nourishes our cells, without doing any damage. But, under stress, when the pressure differentials rise too high, the blood flow inundates our cells, causes retention of fluid. If the stress becomes too intense, the flow can damage our blood vessels, make our heart itself fail.

When the differentials of neural voltages remain moderate, the brain commands our organs without doing any damage to them. But, under stress, when the voltage differentials rise too high, the neural electricity bombards our organs, make them overreact or stall. If stress becomes too intense, the neural electricity can damage our nerves, or cause a burnout to our brain itself.

The same happens for all other flows in our organism. When their driver differentials grow out of proportions, the flows become too intense. They haul our organism. Our body and mind squeak, stagger, and stall.

For a healthy person, a temporary haul does not damage his terrain. If differentials remain too high for too long, the intense flows deform his terrain. The organism loses its ability to return to its point of dynamic equilibrium, on its own.

We cross the zone of stress, and enter the zone of strain.

Stress is different from Strain
What distinguishes 'stress' from 'strain' is this deformation of terrain—the shift of the organism from its zero. Let's understand this phenomenon through a parallel.

Take a piece of eraser. Press it hard and release immediately. The eraser returns to its original shape, its zero point, without any delay.

Now, put the same eraser inside a clamp. Apply stress until the eraser flattens completely, and then release. The eraser takes longer to return to its zero, but it does eventually.

Next, keep the eraser flattened in the clamp for a week. Take it out. It never returns to its zero. The pressure applied has exceeded the eraser's threshold of tolerance, for too long. Its terrain has deformed permanently; the eraser has entered the zone of strain.

An intense pressure, applied for short durations but at regular intervals, will also produce strain in the long term. Once the eraser has strained, it can't return to its zero on its own. A special treatment is required for that to happen.

Our terrain, encompassing all organs, glands, muscles, vessels, nerves, and the mind, also behaves like the eraser under stress.

Moderate stress can deform our terrain, but only temporarily. Our internal mechanism of auto-correction restores our terrain to its point of dynamic equilibrium, once the stress is over. But, if the intensity of stress exceeds the limit of our tolerance, too often or for too long, our terrain deforms, and crosses over to the zone of strain.

External help becomes required to make our organism return to its zero.

The decision to use corrective measures depends on whether we've gone beyond this threshold, between stress and strain. We shall see later how to determine this threshold.

What happens to our flows after strain?
Strain deforms our terrain, disrupts all flows within our organism. Food, blood, lymph, neural electricity, glandular secretion, and excretions—all flow abnormally.

Sixteen channels of vital energy traverse our terrain. Strain deforms them too. Their flows spill over, stagnate, deviate, or stop altogether. Physiological and psychological distress manifest, simultaneously.

A strained terrain is not a disease by itself, but a precursor to it.

Strain induces a vicious cycle, by affecting perception
Strain deforms the meridian of our mind; we perceive normal pressure as excessive.

For a strained terrain, the threshold between stress and strain is lower than what it would have been normally. Consequently, a pressure that will not strain a normal terrain will deform a strained terrain even further.

More the strain instills into our terrain, worse our perception becomes. More our perception degrades, further the strain penetrates into our terrain.

A vicious cycle ensues.

A person with strained terrain has a strained outlook on life. The continual frictions inside reduce his tolerance of pain. He gets sandwiched between external and internal pressures a lot more than others. And, further the strain penetrates his terrain, worse this sandwiching becomes.

How can we raise our threshold of tolerance?
By being Zen.
A Zen person:

    - Treats stress more like a challenge than menace,

    - Has a threshold that's 43% higher than the average.

A Zen person, by living a wholesome life of synergy, increases his robustness and resilience to stress. In chapter 13, we'll see what this 'wholesome living' is.

Signs of stress and strain vary by individual
Stress eliminates slacks from our life, and boosts our performance.

    We should not interfere with our organism, unless stress is pushing us beyond our threshold of tolerance. If strain has already deformed our terrain, we need to take corrective measures, and get the strain out of our organism.

    Earlier we detect strain, quicker we take it out.

How can we detect strain?

In part I, we saw how the symptoms vary, depending on how our organism is handling stress. Signs also vary among individuals, but most fall into one of the three models below.

Model I

An individual from this group has strong digestion and soft authority.

- Under moderate stress, his authority becomes exigent, his digestion falters, and his mood becomes irritable.
- When strain deforms his terrain, he suffers from stomach burns, eczema, and other inflammatory disorders; his mood becomes aggressive and bitter; and his charismatic authority transforms into oppressive tyranny.

Model II

An individual from this group has efficient elimination and healthy imagination.

- Under moderate stress, his creativity becomes prominent, his intestinal transit and diction accelerate, and his movements become nervous.
- When strain deforms his terrain, he has incoherent ideas, has unfounded fears, and suffers from alternation between diarrhea and constipation.

Model III

An individual from this group has great stability and strong immunity.

> - Under moderate stress, he shows excellent attention to details, but puts on weight, and suffers from lethargy.
> - When strain deforms his terrain, he sleeps too much, becomes jealous, accumulates mucus, and has repeated urinary and genital infections.

Stress challenges us. Our organism faces this challenge by putting its best forward. Our biodynamic force boosts too; both our qualities and frailties become more visible.

We can't choose to keep our qualities and throw our frailties. They are two different labels of the same force inside. Nevertheless, we can adopt a strategy to employ our qualities at their best, and to provoke our frailties at their least.

This optimal strategy leads us to our best.

What is that strategy?

> - If we belong to Model I, we should let our natural leadership roll out, but we must not provoke our digestive system or cynicism.

> - If we belong to Model II, we should let our creativity rise high, but we must check our speed and fear.

- If we belong to Model III, we should pay attention to details, but we must not yield to inertia or mucus-producing foods.

Although 'quality' and 'frailty' are different manifestations of the same force inside us, outsiders don't look at this so generously. When we need to influence others, it's always the 'quality' inside us that gets the job done right:

In Hindu mythology, gods and demons originate from the same. As a result, gods also have their defects, and demons also have their virtues. Prajapati, their teacher and father, knows this fact.

One such demon, through virtuous living, becomes extremely strong. He starts taking over territories of gods, and destroying their pleasure gardens. Frightened, the chief god runs to Prajapati.

"Father! Father! The demon is destroying us."

"Go, fight him then." Prajapati frowns. "Don't come running to me."

"But…" The chief god averts his eyes. "We can't fight him, Father. He's too strong."

"Go and live virtuously like him. For one hundred and one years. Then, come back and fight."

"One hundred and one years! None of the gods will be left by then."

That's right, thinks Prajapati. Living in a world, inhabited by demons only…

"There's a way." Prajapati pulls his palm leaves out.

"What? What?" The chief god sits at Prajapati's feet.

"To kill him, you've to do a sacrificial fire." Prajapati's index slides across a leaf, and then stops. "You'll need a priest, though. More virtuous than this demon."

And that's the problem, Prajapati thinks. At this moment, nobody—no man, no god—is even as virtuous as this demon. He runs his fingers through his white mane.

"There's a way out." Prajapati bites his lower lip.

"What? What?" The chief god touches Prajapati's feet.

"Make an appeal to this demon." Prajapati closes the palm leaves. "To his noble sentiments."

"Noble sentiments, Father!" The chief god smirks. "Of the demon?"

"Trust me, he has it." Prajapati narrows his eyes. "He is your other half, right?"

"If you say so, Father." The chief god sighs. "What do I appeal to him for?"

"Ask *him* to be the priest for the fire."

"For his own death?" The chief god drops his jaw. "Father, have you become crazy?"

Prajapati lifts his hand. "Tell him you're doing this to save the world."

"What if he refuses?"

"He won't, if you use the right words."

The fire gets done; the demon, killed; and the pleasure gardens, recovered.

Once again, noble prevails over the evil.

We can convert our frailty into quality

If we are healthy and living in accordance with self, we notice neither our qualities nor our frailties. They become visible only when we are pushed to our limits, to the extremes of our senses and capacities, where extraordinary visions occur for us.

There, at those limits, if we remain Zen, we can mobilize our willpower with robust civic sense, and convert our frailty into quality. What's destructive inside us becomes constructive; we rise to our inherent potential, and become unique.

Three persons I've seen transformed themselves at their limits:

- One into an extraordinary photographer,
- Another into a fervent social worker,
- And yet another into an exceptional entrepreneur.

They not only shifted from destruction to construction, but also distinguished themselves from the rest.

When their destructive force changed face, and joined hands with their constructive force, they caught up with millions of those turning the slow wheel of security, and then bypassed them. This taste of extraordinary success inspired them into a life-style that engaged their qualities at their best, without provoking their frailties again.

They reached their unique greatness.

We *all* enter into discordance with ourselves at some point in life.
We defy our values, and breed internal conflicts. The subsequent
loss of self-respect leads us into an unwholesome life—living
without synergy, within us and with others. Strain sets in our terrain;
our biodynamic force turns destructive, on ourselves and on others.

But, that's not the end of the world.

To recover, we've to ignore the 'destructive' label of our
force, and treat it as a force only. We must remember that, as long as
we have that force inside us, we can convert it into constructive, by
retrieving accordance with self. Then maintain it constructive, by
living a wholesome life of synergy.

We can do this optimally, once we know our threshold for
intervention. And we can determine that threshold by observing our
signs under stress. Those signs depend on our constitution, our
organic makeup.

What makes us up?

10: By knowing our constitution

What makes up Man?

Or, anything else we see? The question troubles Svetaketu, in Chandogya Upanishad.

"Bring me a fig," his father says.

"Here, Sir."

"Split it."

"Done, Sir."

"What do you see?"

"Seeds, Sir. Very fine seeds."

"Divide those seeds."

"Done, Sir."

"Keep dividing. What do you see?"

"Nothing, Sir."

The finest of all is that 'nothing'—the empty space.

Upanishad says a cosmic energy fills that space. It's the same energy that pervades the entire universe, and, when condensed, creates all living and non-living.

Quantum physics says an atom, the tiniest of matter, is composed of a few electrons, protons, and neutrons, and of empty space mostly. An electromagnetic energy fills that space. Via nuclear reactions, even those electrons, protons, and neutrons can be converted into energy.

This happens at the core of our Sun everyday: millions of tons of gas atoms convert into energy, and radiate into the space.

All elements of the universe can be ultimately decomposed into empty space and energy. All are nothing but condensed forms of these two. Whichever viewpoint you adopt on the formation of the universe, Upanishad or Quantum Physics, the most rudimentary ingredients of all living and non-living are emptiness and energy.

Moreover, at the atomic level, all matters are exchangeable.

For example, there is little difference between the carbon atoms from your body and those from a tiger, a tree, or a rock. Upon erosion, they all return to the same pool of atoms, and get recycled, to create other humans, tigers, trees, and rocks. How they combine, determines the form.

The empty space, *ether*, is the first of the five elements in Ayurveda, the ancient medicine from India. From that ether, arise the other four elements: *air*, *fire*, *water*, and *earth*. These five elements combine with the cosmic energy, and create all living and non-living forms.

What differentiates living from non-living?
Life.

What is life?
A form of energy. At death, this energy departs, and living turns into non-living.

In us, life manifests as a dynamic force that generates movements. We call this force *prana* in Ayurveda, a rough equivalent of 'vital energy' in modern physiology.

What we consume—food, oxygen, or sunlight—also have their own *prana*. Within our cells, the fire of cellular digestion extracts these *prana,* and channels them into ours, which then coordinates hundreds of our functions, and maintains billions of our cells.

Our organism stays healthy and alive.

How does our life start?

During fertilization, the *five elements* of the ovum fuse with those of the spermatozoid. The cosmic energy then extends into the ovum just fertilized, and ignites life; the cell division starts.

Upanishad calls this cosmic energy *Brahman*, the Universal Self. The part of the Universal Self captured in the zygote becomes *Atman*, the Individual Self.

Within each cell, this Individual Self blends inseparably with the *five elements*; and it also serves as the envelope of our body and mind.

It's in this inner self where our accordance or discordance registers.

How does our psyche form?

The Universal Self has three basic qualities: motion, balance, and inertia. The Individual Self retains these three qualities within us:

- Motion manifests as our dynamism

- Balance, as our intellect

- Inertia, as our ego

Together, they form our psyche.

The cognitive and the intellectual parts of the mind reside in the brain; the emotional parts, in the heart.

How do the five elements manifest within us?

Ether manifests as our body cavities and spaces in between cells. *Air* manifests as movements of organs and currents. *Fire* manifests as digestion, assimilation, vision, and comprehension. *Water*, as all body fluids; and *earth*, as the seven tissues.

Prana permeates them all, binds them all.

What all these have to do with our well-being?

The key to our well-being is accordance with self—thinking and doing that go with us.

Each Individual Self has *one* fundamental belief that sets it apart from the rest. From this fundamental belief, a set of core values arise, and drive that individual's body and mind. His well-being depends on whether his thoughts and actions remain coherent with this fundamental belief, and with his core values.

Why?

Thoughts and actions raise electromagnetic waves within our self. These waves propagate through our *ether*, and then penetrate into our *air*, *fire*, *water*, and *earth*. These propagations also influence

128

the basic qualities of our mind—motion, balance, and inertia. Thus, they influence our body and mind entirely, at their finest level.

A thought or action, in accordance with our self, raises waves that pass through our *five elements* harmoniously: **The Alchemy of our Well-being!**

On the contrary, a thought or action, in discordance with our self, raises turbulent waves in us.

Our psyche suffers. We lose our dynamism and balance; our intellect weakens; guilt inflates our ego, makes us defensive.

Internal conflicts implant within our unconscious.

These conflicts gnaw, grate, and burn us from within; our *fire* rises. Excess *fire* damages the *water* and *earth* of our terrain. Its threshold of tolerance drops; stress strains us easily.

A strained terrain behaves like a piano out of tune.

Abnormal rhythms develop within us. We over-react or under-react to stimuli that wouldn't have bothered us before.

Why some never get strained under stress?
Stress produces strain on a terrain only when it has stiffened from internal conflicts, which arise out of discordance with self.

I've observed sixty-seven hard-working people who showed no signs of strain. Their faces registered contentment, their bodies looked relaxed, and their movements had no jitters. All showed full absorption in their works, although the pressure seemed intense. The youngest was a musician of twenty-one years; the oldest, a carpenter of seventy-eight.

I asked them how they handled stress at work. The carpenter's words below synthesize the group's response:

"How do I manage stress?" Vincent frowns. "I didn't pop out of my mother's womb with a stress management manual in my mouth. What *is* stress?"

"When you have too much to do. When you don't see the end of your tunnel."

"Oh! You can see I have a lot to do." He puts his tools away. "But my tunnel always shines bright."

"What lights your tunnel?"

"Here." Vincent taps his chest. "Doing this since I'm fifteen. Started with my grandfather. And I won't do anything else."

"Do you choose your assignments?"

"We have a lot of competition these days from those chain-stores." He wipes sawdust from the workbench. "But, I don't give a damn about earning less. I take a work only when it feels right."

"How do you know when it feels right?"

"You ask funny questions, boy. There,"—his index pokes my chest—"it tells you, if a work is right for you or not."

"My heart?"

"Yes, that's where you feel." He picks up his saw. "Work all day, non stop, but, if that work corresponds to you, your heart still beats strong."

"And, if the work doesn't?"

"Slog even two hours per day on that work,"—he aligns the saw with a mark on the board—"and you eat your heart alive."

For people like Vincent, stress remains an illusion.

Pressure challenges them, but never menaces them. Accordance with self has programmed their organism to reject everything that doesn't go with their hearts. Strain never invades their terrain. Without any knowledge of *the five elements* or of the Individual Self, they have discovered the alchemy of well-being.

We want to be like Vincent, render our terrain robust against stress.

As long as what we do remain in accordance with our self, we retain your well-being.

If we have slipped into unwell-being, our terrain has lost some of its robustness, but we can still regenerate it.

But, before taking any corrective measures, we have to first determine whether our terrain really needs repair, by observing whether our signs deviate too far from their norms. We also have to know which triggers derange our terrain. For these, we have to know its constitutional makeup.

The notion of constitution exists in *all* ancient medicines that have considered Man in its ensemble. For demonstration, however, I shall use only the constitutions from Ayurveda.

Ayurvedic reference constitutions

The *five elements* compose our terrain. *Prana*, the life force, flows through it, controls all our functions, maintains the integrity of our body and mind. Proportions of the *five elements* differ from one terrain to another, and determine:

-Our physical and psychological signs, under stress and strain

-Our triggers, for stress and strain.

Ayurveda categorizes our terrain using three reference constitutions:

-Air-type individuals, with mostly *ether* and *air*

-Bile-type, with mostly *fire*

-Catarrh-type, with mostly *water* and *earth*.

We predominantly belong to one of these types, but we also tilt a little toward the other two. The mix of these three types in us, however, remains unique. Hence, the signs of our stress and strain stay unique too, and so do their triggers.

Our constitution evolves, with age and life-style.

The difference between our congenital constitution and our constitution today determines how far our perceptions, thoughts, and actions deviate from their optimal—that is, from our point of dynamic equilibrium.

The only way to know our congenital constitution is by reading the deep pulses, but only an experienced practitioner can do that. You can, however, have a pretty good idea of your constitutional mix today, through the exercise at the end of this chapter.

For preventing energetic disorders, this knowledge usually suffices.

Why do the signs of stress and strain depend on our constitution?
Pressure generates stress within us.

Our organism responds to this stress: it eliminates all slacks, puts our best qualities forward, and boosts our performance. The organism pays a price too. But, if what we do corresponds to our self, the discomforts go unnoticed, and stress never engenders any major problems for us.

Stress induces strain only when discordance with self is present.

Before tampering with this strain, we must make sure that strain has indeed set in our terrain. Not only one's signs of stress and strain differ from those of another person, but also our own signs of stress differ from our own signs of strain.

Why?

Let's return to the alchemy of the *five elements*.

Say, you are a Bile-type individual. When a situation challenges you, you put your best forward. Bile-type's best is *fire*; under stress, *fire* increases in you more than in Air and Catarrh types. *Fire* boosts your comprehension and courage. You grasp the situation and face the challenge.

Vital energy gravitates toward the region that needs it the most. As Bile-type, you draw your strengths mostly from the solar plexus. Under stress, your energy gravitates toward your solar plexus, and takes charge of the challenge. But, your organism pays a tax.

Your digestive organs also draw their energy from the solar plexus. The excess of energy in your solar plexus inundates these organs. They clog. Their enzyme secretion falls, and their movements slow; your digestion and elimination suffer.

Fire causes inflammation. As Bile-type, you get more burning, more sensitivity to light, and more skin rashes than others.

To prevent damage from this excessive *fire*, your auto-correction mechanism steps in and searches for cooler energy. Your taste buds push you toward sweet foods. A moderate consumption of sweets keeps your *fire* from going out of proportion.

Once stress ends, your organism returns to its zero point.

But, if strain has deformed your terrain, this return doesn't happen; rather, your signs deteriorate.

Strain occurs only when discordance exists.

Discordance weakens all your constitutional elements, including *fire*. Weak *fire* confuses your cellular intelligence; your auto-correction mechanism fails. Your organism can no longer tell whether enough sweets have been consumed or not. You abuse on sweets.

Over consumption instills a vicious cycle in you. *Water* and *earth* from sweets combine with *fire,* generate toxins. These toxins increase *fire* in your blood, and you reach out for more sweets.

Toxins circulate in your blood and deposit on the organs; they weaken. Your liver no longer functions optimally—your digestion of fats and sugars suffers, and your cholesterol level goes up.

Your digestive *fire* deteriorates—acidity and bloating occur, even for your habitual foods. Allergies develop.

Your emotional intelligence deteriorates too. You compensate emotional hunger by excess materials—foods and goods. The excess *fire* raises your anger, causes hysteria and violent dreams.

Now, let's reconsider the signs of stress versus strain from the last chapter:

Model I

An individual from this group has strong digestion and soft authority.

- Under moderate stress, his authority becomes exigent, his digestion falters, and his mood becomes irritable.
- When strain deforms his terrain, he suffers from stomach burns, eczema, and other inflammatory disorders; his mood becomes aggressive and bitter; and his charismatic authority transforms into oppressive tyranny.

This corresponds to Bile-type.

Model II

An individual from this group has efficient elimination and healthy imagination.

- Under moderate stress, his creativity becomes prominent, his intestinal transit and diction accelerate, and his movements become nervous.

- When strain deforms his terrain, he has incoherent ideas, has unfounded fears, and suffers from alternation between diarrhea and constipation.

This corresponds to Air-type.

Model III

An individual from this group has great stability and strong immunity.

- Under moderate stress, he shows excellent attention to details, but puts on weight, and suffers from lethargy.

- When strain deforms his terrain, he sleeps too much, becomes jealous, accumulates mucus, and has repeated urinary and genital infections.

This corresponds to Catarrh-type.

Each one of us has a unique mix of these three reference constitutions. Hence, although our signs of stress and strain follow a pattern, they always remain unique.

What triggers stress and strain in our terrain?
Like increases like: *fire* enhances *fire*.

For example, if you are Bile-type, your terrain already has more *fire* than others. Sun, hot baths, closed heat, spicy food, and repressed anger, everything that contains *fire*, triggers more stress inside you, makes your terrain more vulnerable than others.

The sense organs associated with *fire* are the eyes. So, Bile-type's eyes are more sensitive than others. Strong light and visual pollutions, e.g., from advertisements containing deformed images, derange you more than others.

For the three reference constitutions, the main triggers are as follows.

Air-type:

> *Physiological triggers*: too rapid movements, doing too many things at the same time, speaking too much, or eating foods that provoke flatulence
>
> *Psychological triggers*: fear, anxiety, and anticipation
>
> *Climatic triggers*: strong wind

Bile-type:

> *Physiological triggers*: hot bath, excess alcohol, meat, and spices
>
> *Psychological triggers*: repressed anger, hatred or bitterness
>
> *Climatic triggers*: sun, closed heat, strong light, and visual pollution

Catarrh-type:

> *Physiological triggers*: lack of sport, excess sleep and comfort, foods that are too cold or produce mucus

Psychological triggers: jealousy, attachment, and possessiveness

Climatic triggers: humidity

Exercise 11: Determine your Ayurvedic constitution

For each question, choose only the best response. When you're stressed—

Do you:

    A. Go to toilette frequently?

    B. Suffer from indigestion?

    C. Have congestion of fluids and mucus?

Do you feel oppressed in your:

    A. Lower abdomen?

    B. Upper belly?

    C. Chest?

Do(es) your:

    A. Skin and hair become dry?

    B. Skin gets rashes and hair falls?

    C. Your skin and hair become oily?

Your predominant emotion is:

    A. Fear?

    B. Irritability?

    C. Melancholy?

You:

    A. Lose weight?

    B. Don't change weight?

    C. Gain weight?

Your:

    A. Memory declines?

    B. Oppression of yourself and others increases?

    C. Attachment to goods and people increases?

You:

    A. Wake up between 3 and 5 am?

    B. Wake up between 1 and 3 am?

    C. Have difficulty leaving bed?

Your dreams become:

    A. Too moving?

    B. Violent?

    C. Full of longings?

You:

    A. Speak faster?

    B. Grind your teeth?

    C. Lose your voice?

You move:

    A. Faster?

B. With jitters?

C. With dragging efforts?

You:

    A. Add more items on your task list?

    B. Micro-control everything?

    C. Lose your dynamism?

Your stress becomes worse on:

    A. Windy days?

    B. Hot days?

    C. Cold days?

The percentages of A, B, and C in your response represent, approximately, the proportions of Air, Bile, and Catarrh in your constitution. For a more accurate estimation, include the following steps.

Look at your tongue in the mirror.

Is it:

    A. Thin?

    B. Normal?

    C. Swollen?

Is it red:

    A. At the back?

    B. In the middle and on sides?

C. In the front?

Does it have a coating:

    A. At the back?

    B. In the middle?

    C. In the front?

Now, check your pulse.

    Extend your left hand palm up. Bring the index, middle, and the ring finger of your right hand together, then place them on the outer edge of the left wrist—the ring finger of your right hand should be just below the wrist bone of your left hand. With a light but firm pressure, feel the pulses on the fingertips of your right hand.

Which one dominates:

    A. The ring?

    B. The middle?

    C. The index?

Recalculate the percentages of A, B, and C in your responses.

An Ayurvedic practitioner examines your tongue and reads your constitutional pulses for other reasons too.

    For example, pulses have many levels.

    The deep pulse shows your congenital biodynamic force, whereas the superficial pulse shows your present biodynamic force.

The difference between the two shows the extent of discordance within you.

It also shows the deviation between who you are, and who you're meant to be.

Exercise 12: Re-examine your signs of stress

In part I, you've identified your signs of stress. In this part, you've seen whether these signs fall under a pattern. You've also made a preliminary judgment on whether to take corrective measures or not. Now, reexamine these signs in the light of your constitutional makeup, whether they correspond to stress or strain.

Step 1: Take the percentages of A, B, and C that you've just calculated. Say, your constitution is made of 50% Bile, 25% Air, and 25% Catarrh.

Step 2: Now, take the signs of stress and strain, corresponding to these three constitutions, from the section 'Ayurvedic reference constitutions'.
Do your signs correspond, approximately, 50% of the time to Bile-type, 25% of the time to Air-type, and 25% of the time to Catarrh-type?

Step 3: Now, compare your signs between stress and strain.

If your signs correspond more frequently to those of 'stress', you don't need any corrective measures.

Just remain aware of your personal triggers of stress, from the section 'What triggers stress and strain in our terrain?'. Roughly speaking, for your constitution, the triggers corresponding to the 'Bile' will affect you twice more than the triggers corresponding to 'Air' and 'Catarrh'.

If your signs, however, correspond more frequently to those of 'strain', you need to take corrective measures, and reestablish your well-being.

Strain occurs only under discordance.

Hence, to correct strain, you've to start by retrieving your accordance.

11: By recovering our fundamental belief

To restore our well-being, first we need to reestablish accordance with ourselves.

The door to our inner self opens with a key belief. In discordance, we bury this key under stress.

The loss of this key separates us from our core, deviates us from our optimal actions, reactions, and perceptions. But the key is not lost for ever. We can retrieve it, and open the door to our self again.

The exercises we've done so far to approach our core, have already brought us closer to this key, but unconsciously. Now, we have to do the rest consciously, by recoiling from our context, by observing our thoughts and actions in the three spheres of life—our inner self, our immediate surrounding, and our external world.

Why?

Our thoughts and actions are guided by a set of values, embedded deeply within us.

These core values arise from the fundamental belief that distinguishes our Individual Self from the rest. By observing our thoughts and actions, we deduce these values that guide our mind and body. Then we synthesize them, and arrive at our fundamental belief.

The door to our self opens again.

Case Study I

Patrick, 26 years old, investment banker on fast-track, attends a workshop on conflict management. At the end, he is to receive feedback from Clifford, the organizer of the workshop.

Patrick walks into Clifford's office, reluctantly.

"In the individual sessions, your performance was topnotch." Clifford's lips part in an attempt to smile, but his eyes stay cold.

Fake. Patrick dismisses his remark.

"But, in the group sessions,"—Clifford rotates the pen in between his fingers, then stops— "your interactions were somewhat strained."

Let it be. Patrick is running out of patience with this workshop. He has been away from work for a week already; and from his family too. Why does his bank keep putting him through these stupid seminars?

Clifford drums his fingers on an open file.

"You socialized very little in groups." He turns two pages in the file. "Seems to happen the same way within your firm, but—"

"Why don't you go straight to the point?" Patrick sighs.

Clifford frowns. "Your rapport with clients is excellent, though."

"The clients count the most, right?" Patrick wants to explode.

"True. That's why you've come up so far in your job. And, so quickly." Clifford scans Patrick's face. "The question is: are you happy within your firm?"

"Happy? What does it mean to be happy?"

Clifford pushes the file away. "Do you enjoy your client work?"

"Let's say, I bring in enough money for the bank."

"What about the rest?"

"What about it?"

"Do you enjoy being in your firm?"

"Why?" Patrick fidgets. "What's there in that file?"

"Not much." Clifford looks over his glasses. "But, I believe, you could handle authority there a lot better."

He takes his glasses off.

"Don't get me wrong, Patrick. Your boss is really impressed how you handle conflicts at your clients' sites."

And, of course, his boss is *not* impressed how he handles conflicts within his firm: go for a head butt, or avoid completely.

"That's why I'm here, Clifford." Patrick slings his arm over the back of his chair. "To learn how to manage conflicts, effectively."

Clifford leans forward. "Then, let's talk about our framework. Do you think it—"

"Enough!" Patrick lifts his hand. "The workshop is over."

"What are you taking back from us?"

"Tell you what." Patrick swings his arm forward, and sits upright. "Those matrices are real pretty. Even impressive. But they do nothing, when the source of the conflict is inside—"

"Inside your firm."

"Just forget it." Patrick blows. These people are so stuck with their theories on firms and their frameworks; they'll never understand what's really eating him up from inside.

"Sorry, I interrupted you." Clifford scratches his neck.

"Never mind. It's no longer important."

Clifford looks at him intently. "What's bothering you, Patrick? I mean, about your firm?"

This guy has been paid to probe. He won't let go, until he has something. Patrick smacks his lips. "What's bothering me is that I need this job."

"Because, it pays well?"

"Yes." Patrick startles. "I wouldn't have thought like this before, but I do now."

"The firm needs you too." Clifford wipes his glasses. "Your skills, your expertise, your contacts… Isn't that a fair exchange?"

"Right. Money for service. Enough to be happy in life."

Clifford rolls his chair forward. "How can I help you, Patrick?"

"Frankly, you can't." Patrick squeezes the muscles of his neck. "Sorry, I don't think anybody can help me in my situation." His voice chokes. He presses his lips together, tightly. No way is he going to cry before this guy.

"Among your assignments,"—Clifford leans on his elbows— "is there one you particularly enjoy?"

"Yes, communication." Patrick inhales deeply. "Honest and transparent." He taps his knuckles on the desk. "And, not waste my life away, politicking."

These days, up in the ladder of ranks, Patrick is being forced to dip his nose, deeper and deeper, into the firm politics. Honesty and transparency have fallen aside, altogether.

But, who is to blame, other than himself?

He is the one who abandoned journalism in college, and took this banking job. Well, to some extent, he felt obliged to do that— Mom and the younger siblings would have been on the street otherwise.

Nevertheless, he could have changed job, once things got better. But, no!

"The firm values you, Patrick." Clifford puts his glasses on. "Have you tried switching job within your firm?"

"Like what?"

"A communication specialist may be?"

"I can't." Now, he has his palace to pay for, two thousand pounds a month, plus his children's elite private school. Only if he hadn't given into all that, but it's too late now. Just go back home, and continue as before, till death takes you out of this trap.

Clifford juts his chin. "The issues you have arise when you know you're not operating at your best." He clears his throat. "Because, you know, your job doesn't correspond to you."

The words stab Patrick. He doesn't want his colleagues to discover his lack of passion at work—that's why he either shoves

148

them or shuns them. But, can others see his feelings so easily? His face feels hot. He takes out his handkerchief, and wipes his face.

Probably, most don't. This guy has been trained to do this work. And, he seems willing to help. Why not give him a chance?

"What's the remedy then?" Patrick loosens his tie, and wipes his neck.

"Choose a job that corresponds to you." Clifford closes the file. "Not just to feed you, but to make you feel whole."

"What kind of a job is that?" Patrick clutches the armrests.

Clifford glances at Patrick's hands. "One that has synergy with you."

"And, what will that synergy do?"

"You and your job will reinforce each other."

Patrick drops his hands on the lap. "Is there such a job?"

"Always." Clifford leans on his forearms. "In my twenty-eight years of service, I've never come across someone who tried sincerely, and couldn't find that job. There's a right job for everyone in this world."

Outside Clifford's office, Patrick opens his notebook. He turns to a section tagged 'external' and writes:

'Friction with others arises when you know you're not operating at your best, when you know your job doesn't correspond to you.'

'When you're unhappy at your work, you're not at ease with your colleagues.'

'When a job corresponds to you, you and your job reinforce each other.'

'There is a right job for everyone in this world.'

For the last seven months, Patrick has been taking notes.

Nobody will understand his feelings at work. Writing helps to express those, at least to himself. At the beginning, those notes looked haphazard, but now a pattern is emerging out of them.

He turns to a section tagged 'internal' and writes:

'Conflicts within me, conflicts with others.'

The words ring a bell. He goes back a few pages:

'Angry with myself, angry with others.'

'Uneasy with myself, uneasy with others.'

Everything seems to come from within.

Three years pass.

At 29, Patrick has a heart attack at the airport. His doctor prescribes him a month of recovery, away from work and home. His wife, Tessa, comes to see him at his sanatorium in the Alps.

"Now what?" Patrick leans back against the headboard.

Tessa sits next to him. "It was time for you to leave that job."

He stares at her face. "What will happen to the rest of you?"

"Nothing worse than if you went."

"At least, you'd have received money from my life insurance." He looks out through the window.

"Stop thinking about money!" She squeezes his arm. "Your company is working out an exit package for you. We'll look for something that suits you better."

"Something?" He shakes his head. "I wanted to be a journalist, Tessa."

"Be then!" Her gaze pierces his eyes. "Now."

"Those jobs don't pay much." He pushes her arm away. "Who would look after our finances?"

"The same one who would have looked after, if you went."

He tilts his head backward. "Don't you all depend on me?"

"No, Patrick." She sighs. "We support each other, but we don't depend on you." Her forehead creases, and her eyes lower. "I don't know how to…"

She has repeated those words so many times before. Today, seeing her at the end of her rope, he lets them sink into him. And, they swell his guilt.

He takes her hand. "Tessa, I've been so heavy for all these years. So picky, so pushy about everything."

"That's okay, Patrick." She cocks her head. "You've improved over time."

"Really?" He thought he only became worse.

She nods. "You'll keep getting better."

He turns toward her. "You think?"

"You're not the same person anymore." She fixes her gaze on his forehead. "Take a stock of yourself, and you'll see."

That's what he has been doing since he came here. But, he didn't feel he has changed. The heart attack took him to the edge, and showed him the abyss beyond. That awful sight—could that have changed him? Or, his vision at least?

He hopes Tessa is right. The thought sends a current of warmth through him. He pushes the bed-sheet off his legs, and sits upright.

"Tessa, I had a dream few nights ago."

"About what?"

"I was a planet up there." He points to the ceiling. "And you all rotated around me, like satellites. Attached to me, by strings."

She laughs. "Come on, Patrick. Satellites are not attached to their planet by strings." She reaches for his cheek. "Gravity keeps them together."

She is right! How stupid he has been to think like that. Well, it was a dream after all. But, nevertheless, a strange dream.

"We rotate around each other, but freely." She holds his chin up. "It's love that keeps us together." She rubs his chest. "Stop taking the entire burden of the family on you. You're not alone."

"Wouldn't our family have fallen apart, if I went?"

She bites her lips. "No, Patrick. We would have reorganized ourselves differently." Her chest swells. "There is something bigger that holds us together."

The last phrase echoes within him. Where has he heard it before? Not recently. Not from her at least.

"You didn't go, Patrick." She turns his face toward her. "That means—it wasn't the time for you to go." She pats his chest. "The heart attack was a message for all of us: for you, to change job; and, for us, to change life."

A weight lifts off him. He closes his eyes and takes a deep breath.

"Get up, my man." She lifts his hands. "And pull yourself together. I have an address for you."

After Tessa leaves, Patrick writes in his notebook:

'Gravity holds planets, love holds family.'

'We support each other, but not depend on each other.'

'I have changed.'

Has he? Most probably. Why would Tessa lie? He continues his notes:

'Something bigger holds us together.'

He stops. The phrase resonates in him again, but he still can't see from where. He scratches his head, and then moves on:

'I didn't go because it wasn't the time for me to go.'

'The heart attack was a message for all.'

He turns the pages back and forth, scans his notes. He compares them, before and after the heart-attack.

They look so different, feel so different. Their tone and content have changed so sharply after the accident. Even their appearance has changed—from scribbling, to neat writing.

Tessa is right. He has changed indeed.

Returning home, Patrick took appointment with Stuart, an osteopath in his late sixties, who also practices herbal medicine. His bank agreed on an exit package, which would cover his expenses for four months. He launched his job search in journalism.

Today is his third session with Stuart. After interviewing with a financial magazine, Patrick enters Stuart's clinic.

"How did your interview go?" Stuart closes the door behind him.

Patrick sits on the sofa, and puts his attaché case on the lap. "They've made me an offer." He hesitates, then takes the attaché off his lap, and stands it at his feet.

Stuart notices his moves. "You felt at ease with them."

"You can say that." Patrick leans back. "I didn't hide anything from them."

Stuart walks to the file cabinet. "You mean your lack of motivation in the last job?"

"Yes." Patrick pushes the attaché case away from his feet. "And, that was such a relief!" He exhales.

"Do you sleep better now?" Stuart opens a drawer and picks up a hanging folder.

"Well, not exactly. But I have no nightmares anymore." Thank god! "I still sweat quite a bit though."

Stuart turns toward him. "When?"

"Toward the end of the night."

"How is your digestion?"

"Lot less acidity. No more winds. Those plants are working, but…" His health still has quite a distance to cover.

Stuart stops near the sofa. "Something bothers you still?"

"Yeah, my headaches." Patrick dents his temples. "If I didn't get these damn headaches, I could have done so much more."

"Patrick, you're still treating yourself harshly."

"Won't you, if for all these years, your body hasn't cooperated with you?" Neither has his mind.

"But, it *is* now." Stuart touches his shoulder. "So, be gentler."

"Look at these!" Patrick clasps a fold of fat on his belly. "They make me feel like a sloth. I just—" He senses Stuart's gaze upon him, and looks up.

Stuart has stopped moving.

"Sorry." Patrick searches for words.

Stuart nods. And his eyes radiate compassion.

Patrick shrugs. "I remember what you said." He sits upright. "If I want to improve, I must first accept the way I'm now. That was so hard at first, but now I—" He chokes, turns his face away from Stuart.

"You've done it, finally."

"I'm still trying, but… I can be tough with myself sometimes."

"You're doing your best." Stuart sits at his desk. "You changed your diet. You're exercising again. We'll think of other ways to improve your life-style."

Healthy life-style isn't new to Patrick. His parents always had it at home.

He continued to live healthy, throughout the university, even through the early years at the bank. But then pressure built up. Frustration darkened his world. And he hated himself—his body, mind, and life-style. He let everything degenerate.

Now, out of that dark hole, he's seeing the ray of life again.

He has started to like himself, but not love yet. A healthier lifestyle is becoming easier, but not entirely natural. He slips at times, but Stuart and Tessa help him back on track. He is so lucky to have them around. He's going to stand up to the challenge.

He looks up. "Why did my body and mind turn against me so violently?"

"You must have forced yourself into doing something that didn't go with you at all." Stuart comes around and stands before him. "Let me take your pulse."

True. The banking job didn't feel a hundred-percent right for him, but he hadn't accepted that job against his will either. Not totally. Given the circumstances at that time, he had acted logically.

Stuart watches his face. "You must have gone against your fundamental belief." He lets Patrick's wrist go.

Patrick startles. "My fundamental belief?"

"One that guides you in everything." Stuarts walks to his desk.

Patrick watches his steps. "What could that be?"

"You'll know." Stuart sits in his chair. "Each person has one, usually planted by someone close."

Patrick was close to his dad, very close indeed. And Dad had his theories, but they didn't work, not in Patrick's case at least. That's why he set them aside, took that banking job. It's unlikely any of those theories formed his fundamental belief.

Does he have a fundamental belief?

Stuart leans forward. "That belief drives you, Patrick. When you go with that belief, your body and mind become your best friends."

And, when you don't, they become your worst enemies. Who could have witnessed that better than Patrick?

Does that mean he has a belief indeed?

When he accepted the banking job, something scraped his heart. And the wound hurt for months afterward. Could that have come from contradicting his belief?

May be, after all, he has a belief.

Stuart points to Patrick's chest. "Now your actions must conform to that belief. That's why your body and mind are cooperating with you."

"Will I ever know that belief?"

"You will, but at its time."

If his actions correspond to his belief now, he can't be far from it. He can certainly do something, to get there faster. "What can I do?"

"Just follow your acts. Feel what they do to you."

That's what Patrick has been doing—studying his own actions—even before he met Stuart. Who pushed him to take notes, to reflect upon them?

"How do I know I'm doing the right thing?"

His own words stir him. He has heard them somewhere, long ago.

Who said those? To whom? And why did they come out of his mouth now?

He closes his eyes. A series of tangled words pass before him, but he can't decipher them. He feels Stuart's gaze upon him again, and opens his eyes.

"You were frowning, Patrick." Stuart beams. "You're on the right track, but don't strain yourself. Let your belief return to you, on its own."

Later, Patrick writes in his notebook:

'You're driven by a fundamental belief. All your values, all your forces arise from that belief.'

'When you don't go with that belief, your body and mind become your worst enemies.'

He stops. Why can't he think positive? Leave the past behind?
He crosses out that phrase and writes:

'When you go with that belief, your body and mind become your best friends.'

That feels a lot better. He continues:

'Your body and mind are cooperating with you now. Be gentler with them.'

'When you hate yourself, your body and mind degenerate.'

The past really holds onto you, huh!
He crosses the last phrase out, and writes:

'When you love yourself, your body and mind regenerate.'

He crosses out a few more negative statements, and then moves on:

'Your fundamental belief is never destroyed. You can retrieve it by following your acts.'

He leans back and stares at his list of points.
Too long! If he wants to get something useful out of them, he must cut. But, not today.

His intuition is right, though. He can't be far from his fundamental belief. Flickers of it have already passed through his mind, several times. But, he'll listen to Stuart now. He'll let that belief rise, on its own.

He *is* going to be patient this time.

Patrick accepts the offer from the financial magazine, to join them in fall. For the summer, he goes back to his hometown in the US. After his vacation, he returns to see Stuart.

When he walks in, Stuart is wiping a framed photo, of a couple and two kids. The man in the photo looks like Stuart's son.

Patrick hesitates. "Are they your grand-children?"

"Yes, they live in Sidney." A paternal smile spreads across Stuart's face.

"I haven't been a good boy this summer." Patrick stretches his arm over the back of the sofa. "I stopped taking those plants."

"Good. You don't need them anymore." Stuart places the photo on his desk. "How was summer?"

"Took a month off, saw Mom back home. The kids came with me too. Tessa joined us two weeks later."

"What did you do before she came?"

"Took the kids to a vacation camp, by the sea. That was something!" Patrick rubs his neck.

Stuart takes his glasses off.

Patrick shifts. "Before, I would control every movement of my kids. And, if they didn't listen—"

"Tell me what you did in that camp, Patrick."

"Sorry." Patrick straightens his back. "Just got up, followed what the kids did."

"How did it go?"

"That was a real surprise for them."

"And, for you?"

"A lot of fun."

"You discovered the kid inside you?"

Patrick flings his hand over the head. "Tessa said, 'Those games, Patrick, you would have never allowed to our kids.'"

Stuart presses his lips together, tightly.

Patrick sighs. Alright. Leave that route altogether.

"You know, Stuart." Patrick sways his knees. "Something changed drastically about my social life."

Stuart lifts his chin.

"In my high school, I had friends. But, when going got hard,"—Patrick cracks his knuckles—"I became too demanding on them. And, they disappeared."

He smacks his lips. "In their place, a bunch of complainers thumped into my life."

Stuart's gaze remains steady on Patrick.

"Tessa would call them 'leeches', but I clung to them for life."

Stuart touches his chin, but still says nothing.

"Then guess what happened?" Patrick slides to the edge of the sofa. "During our vacation in the US, I couldn't find their numbers on my list of contacts."

Patrick sweeps his hand. "Tessa had erased them all, before I left."

Stuart smiles. "Did you make new friends?"

"I would have tried, but Mom said: 'Pat. Friends meant for you, show up by themselves. You can't search for them.'"

"With such friends, one plus one exceeds two. But, you have to leave them to the chances."

Chances! That's it. Patrick's heart screams. Dad would—

"Let's change the subject." Stuart leans forward. "Have you given some thoughts to your new job?"

"No, not yet." Patrick scratches his head. "It stirs my passion. So I'll be fine, I think."

"Passion *may* lead to illusion. We need to guard against that."

"I know, I know." Patrick lifts his hand. "When I was at school, I idealized those journalists. Then, in my banking job, we did initial public offering for two media companies. That broke all my illusions about journalism."

Stuart pushes his glasses over the head. The intensity in his eyes centers Patrick.

"Alright, alright. There were other benefits from that banking job too." Patrick rubs his face. "Like my maturity, for example. And that has stayed with me, even after I left them."

Patrick runs his thumb along the seam of his trouser. "But, with my energy, I'll add more value to journalism than banking."

His own words take him by surprise. He repeats them in his head.

Stuart leans on his elbows. "Spend your energy, in a cause, that *you* believe is worthy."

The phrase jolts Patrick.

Those words! So many years later!

His heart leaps.

That night, after Tessa and the children slept, Patrick sneaks into the kitchen.

Right after his session with Stuart, he was too shaken to take notes. Now, he writes in his notebook:

'There is still a kid inside me.'

'With true friends, one plus one exceeds two.'

'You can't plan such friendships; you've to leave them to the chances.'

'Bad experiences aren't all bad; they always serve something.'

'Spend your energy in what *you* think is worthy.'

The last phrase makes him shudder.

Patrick doesn't believe in supernatural stuff, but how did Dad's words come out of Stuart's mouth?

Goose bumps prickle his forearms. He stands up and pours a glass of water.

He has come close to his fundamental belief, but doesn't know how. Now he has to do the rest, by himself. Patrick puts the glass down, and flips through his notes.

So much! He is going to have to select, and trim them. He can, now.

He arranges his notes in two categories: 'external', and 'internal'.

Within each category, he crosses out all incidental remarks, combines similar points, and shortens them. Then he copies those phrases on two separate sheets, one for each category, and pushes his notebook away.

He stares at the two sheets.

The phrases have more punch. And they make more sense too.

He is coming closer.

On another sheet he writes two headings: 'In agreement', and 'In disagreement'. Then he starts writing those points under them.

Some don't fit under either.

But, there is a pattern of coherence among them. He adds a third heading called 'Chances' to the right, and finishes organizing the points in three columns.

The middle column looks the longest. The phrases there make him cringe.

In disagreement with one's fundamental belief, one disintegrates from within. One has too much to suffer, too much to complain. He presses his fist against the mouth, and sucks on the knuckles. Then, he writes under that column:

'Disagreement leads you to degeneration. And then, to painful death.'

He tosses the pen and grabs the glass. He guzzles the water down, and clanks the empty glass on the table. His index quivers on the rim of the glass, and his gaze remains fixed on the sheet.

His finger stops.

He reaches inside a drawer and pulls out a scissor. He chops the middle column off, and places the other two next to each other. He leans back, clasps his hands behind the head, and looks at the ceiling.

Yes. When you do things in line with your belief, all become effortless. Patrick writes under the left column:

'In agreement, you operate at your best.'

The right column under the heading 'Chances' looks mysterious. Someone's hand has been present all along his life. Underneath that column, he writes Tessa's words:

'We're supported by something bigger than us.'

Below, he writes his father's words, echoed by Stuart:

'Put your energy in what you consider worthy.'

Something binds these last three phrases. He must be pretty close.

His heart beats faster. He jumps from his chair and opens the window. He closes his eyes, fills his lungs, and lets the three phrases crawl under his eyelids.

Then his mind blanks. And the words merge…

He swings back to the table and writes:

'There is a force that binds us all. Do your part, wholeheartedly, and leave the rest to this force.'

He stops.

He places the pen at the bottom of the sheet, and looks at the two phrases he has just written. They fit so well with the rest.

He has reached 'home' now.

He won't lose his path again.

Case Study II

Life-threatening events crush our illusions, shove us toward our inner self. We retrieve what's truly important to us: our fundamental belief.

What if we haven't had such dramatic turning points?

We can still retrieve our belief—by observing our actions, particularly around the milestones of our life. But, we must change our point of view drastically, by moving as far away as possible from our habitual context.

Sophie, 38 years old, management consultant, did this change with a month-long solitary stay, in a deserted forest bungalow.

"The first two days were such a relief." She blows a large puff of air. "No grinding, no complaining, no squeezing for deadlines. But, then…"

Her fingers tremble. "Then, on the third day, a deep hollow opened up within me." The whites of her eyes bulge. "Like I was sinking in a well of melancholy."

"Did you cry?"

"Oh, yes." Her forehead creases. "And the sadness passed."

"What came out?"

"Those stupid things I did in my adolescence." Her eyes roll. "And, how I came out of them."

"How?"

She swallows. "Some people helped me, of course. But, I came out mostly by *my* own efforts."

"Your reward for looking back!"

She nods. "Then I thought: if I could help myself then, I can certainly help myself better now."

She pushes a fringe of hair over the ear. "So, on the fourth day, I started writing things down. Like, my thoughts. My actions, reactions, and perceptions in the three spheres of life, as you asked me to do."

Sophie's glitch is her sarcasm.

Sarcasm has destroyed her marriage, has alienated her friends and colleagues, and is making her son rebel today. She can't move anywhere without raising animosity, and she claims she can do nothing about it.

Let's see how she resolved this problem, by recovering her fundamental belief.

In her personal sphere, she writes:

'I'm not good at drawing presentation slides. Forcing me to draw them causes frustration, wastes time and energy; the quality of my presentation suffers.'

'I don't like too many numbers. Forcing me to focus on them alone causes tension and confusion; the quality of my work suffers.'

She has synthesized the two statements into:

'Rubbing on weaknesses hurts performance, and depresses mood.'

Her notes in personal sphere continue:

'I grasp the core issues quickly, and formulate an overall strategy early in the project. That gives me an expansive feel, and the next steps roll in efficiently.'

'I ask the right questions, and listen to understand my clients. They become open to my influence, and that makes working with them a lot easier.'

'I write clear and concise recommendations. They inspire my clients, and that gives me a sense of achievement.'

She has synthesized the three statements into:

'Embracing strengths boosts performance, and elevates mood.'

On the next page, she has copied the two synthetic statements side-by-side, and written below them:

'To improve your performance and mood, focus on your strengths.'

In her immediate surrounding, she writes about her son:

'Harsh words make Paul do his homework worse.'

'Firm but polite words make him work better.'

About her ex-husband, she writes:

'Jacques listened and cooperated, when I spoke to him inspiringly.'

'Jacques still listened, but did nothing, when I spoke to him negatively.'

'Jacques left me, the week after I was sarcastic with him before my parents.'

About her colleagues and friends, she writes:

'When I show consideration for their unintended errors, they show gratitude, and correct those errors enthusiastically. And they stand by me later.'

'When I corner them with criticisms, they may admit and correct their errors, but with a lot of resentments. And then they move away from me.'

Her synthesis in the immediate surrounding goes:

'To encourage people, approach them constructively.'

About her external world, she writes:

'When I overtake people in rush, they curse. I gain 10 seconds, but a bitter feeling lingers over me.'

'When I let people overtake me, they thank. I lose 30 seconds, but feel lighter inside.'

'When I enter a tense room smiling, the tension dissolves. People thank silently, and become receptive to me.'

Her synthesis in the external world goes:

'To smoothen your way through others, use generosity.'

On the page over, she has copied the three synthetic phrases, from the three spheres:

'To improve your performance and mood, focus on your strengths.'

'To encourage people, approach them constructively.'

'To smoothen your way through others, use generosity.'

Below, she writes:

'What all these have in common?'

In a box under, she writes:

'Positive works better than negative.'

She has recovered her fundamental belief.

Sophie entered into discordance with her belief at a mentoring workshop.

"Keep reminding what needs to be improved," her mentor said. "That's the only way to achieve distinction."

Sophie kept up with her reminders—to herself, to her husband, to her son, to her colleagues, and to everyone who crossed her—for what needed to be improved. She forgot to remind, herself and others, what was already good.

Under pressure, her reminders took the form of biting criticism, but she wasn't aware of that. She was surprised when people didn't thank her for those reminders, or ignored her progressively. When her urgent tone no longer worked, she took to sarcasm, and people moved away from her.

Then her own sarcasm turned upon her, but she couldn't escape from herself.

During her month-long solitary stay, she disconnected herself totally from all these, and recovered her fundamental belief.

But, something else also helped.

"My history teacher at school would say: 'Positive works better than negative.'" Sophie flips a page in her diary. "At that age, those words seemed strange, but I started doing experiments."

"Like what?"

"Every time I spoke to my friends positively, they listened. And, every time I criticized them, or pushed them too hard, they just went away."

"Did your parents put a lot of pressure on you, to improve?"

"Dad was in the military." She pushes the bangs off her eyes. "Anyway, I started talking to my brother encouragingly. Even to Mom sometimes, when she went out of hand. And it worked!"

"Did it work with your dad too?"

"I wouldn't know." She bites her lips. "He went one day, and never returned."

"Did you research your favorite stories?"

"Yes, I did." She lays four books on the sofa.

"What's the common theme among them?"

"Positive always wins over the negative."

"An overworked cliché, that still pays in different ways."

"I took these books with me to vacation." She straightens the corners of one. "In that period of horrible emptiness, I started flipping through them."

She puts the book on her lap. "Within minutes, I entered a different world. A world I had left aside for a long time."

"What did you extract from there?"

"My values." She raises her diary. "Then I asked myself: 'What could lead me to those values?' And I saw my core belief."

"Do you keep a lot of books?"

"No! But, these four books,"—she brushes their jackets— "I've kept them since my teenage years."

"Why?"

"What's in them must correspond to me."

Nine out of ten have their fundamental belief formed before the age of fifteen. These beliefs are always simple and short, like:

'Diligence enables you to bear success with grace.'

'When you help others, you also help yourself.'

'When you go too fast, you end your life before others.'

Lean and clean, they fit better with our self.

12: By reconstructing our well-being

The moment we recover our fundamental belief, we open the door to our self. At this point, 91% of my clients experience a profound release within.

As soon as we're in line with our belief, further damage to our terrain stops immediately. Convalescence sets in via the *five elements*. Then we've do the rest, by aligning ourselves with our values in the three spheres of life.

That's how we finalize our original solution.

The recovery of the fundamental belief is an inward journey; the finalization of our solution, an outward.

Finalize your original solution in steps
You've already worked out your original solution twice before. Now, let's refine it through the following steps.

Reinforce your fundamental belief and identify your core values
On a fresh sheet of paper, write your fundamental belief at the top.

The core values that guide you arise from this belief. Underneath, write the values you count upon the most.

For example, Patrick from the last chapter writes for his belief:

A binding force holds us together, as long as we do our part right.

For his core values, he writes:

- Put your energy where you feel it serves the best.
- Do your part, honest and straightforward, even if it's not the most convenient.
- Maintain health & autonomy of your body and mind.
- Allow freedom to your family, to do their parts right.

Identify the changes in the three spheres of your life

You might have already identified them. Here, in the light of your fundamental belief and core values, prioritize them. Let's start with elimination.

In each sphere, look at the items at the bottom of your list.

Can you let some of those sort out by themselves?

Yes. Do it.

For example, Patrick writes:

In the sphere of self

1. Work and live under zero regrets and resentments
2. Boost metabolism, join a swimming club
3. Each time posture stoops, straighten; open up. See what happens to your mood
4. Play saxophone at least one night per week. Later, join a class and hone skills
5. Recover the health of your heart

In the immediate surrounding

1. Free Tessa from cooking, at least two evenings a week

2. Follow children's wishes, one day per weekend

3. Move house to an area with more parks and less bars

4. New mortgage must not exceed one third of disposable income

5. In new job, have lunch with colleagues twice a week

6. Get to know the new manager at personal level

7. Make new friends along a line of true passion

He scrutinizes the list and crosses out point 7. In swimming and music classes, he would make new friends automatically.

He rethinks points 5 and 6.

If he had lunch with his colleagues, he would automatically know his manager at a social level. If he did any further efforts to know his manager personally, he would overdo it. Moreover, his colleagues could become jealous or suspicious.

He crosses out point 6.

In the external world

1. Zero judgment of strangers

2. Zero frustration about the uncontrollable

3. Zero fault-finding with others

4. Change criticism to indifference

5. Act out of compassion toward others

6. Don't try to win a conflict

7. In a conflict, remain centered on the issue, not on the person

8. In a conflict, also know what's important for the other

9. Accept the rights and perspectives of others

10. Don't try to change the world

Points 1, 2, and 3 imply 4; he crosses out point 4.

Point 1 implies 3; he crosses out point 3.

Point 9 implies 8; he crosses out point 8.

Point 7 implies 6; he crosses out 6.

Points 2 and 9 imply 10; he crosses out point 10.

Now he looks at the surviving points, in the three spheres of life together. They'll improve the health of his heart automatically.

He crosses out point 5, in the sphere of self.

Make changes in stages

Once you've identified the changes you want to make, implement them in stages.

Know your constraints in each sphere. Make a plan with concrete stages, allowing sufficient time for each. Then implement those stages, with a flexible attitude.

For example, Patrick decides:

In the sphere of self

1. By nine months, swim 20 laps at a stretch. But, start with 2 laps, then keep adding 1 per week. In 3 months, join a swimming club.

2. Haven't played saxophone in 17 years. Go easy; try 1 song per week. After 3 favorite songs, join a class.

3. Every time you don't regret or resent something, congratulate yourself. If you slip, don't become angry. Instead, see what positive comes out of that negative.

In the immediate surrounding

1. By the end of next week, free Tessa one evening from cooking. Next Saturday, do what the children wish.

2. Meet new colleagues twice before starting. Devote one meeting to the human issues at work, and our social lives.

3. Before starting at the new job, sell house and move. Put the house on sell in two weeks, and finish shopping for mortgage by the end of month. Then start looking for a new house.

In the external world

1. Once per day, smile at those who walk over your toes. Watch their reactions. Don't get bitter, if they return your smile with a grimace.

2. When the desire to criticize invades, stop. See the positive. Then say it, if dealing with a person. Or, write it down, if dealing with an event.

3. Once per week, find something ugly. Then, keep looking at it, until a beautiful trait shows up on it.

4. When the desire to micro-control hits, withdraw. See how things settle by themselves.

5. When someone insults you, ignore. If the person seems worthy, focus on the issue at hand, and divert conflict into collaboration.

At the end, Patrick writes:
> Be flexible.
> Always leave margin for errors.
> Dignity implies civility.

Adjust attitude inside out

Attitude plays a crucial role in recovery.

Negative attitude secretes adrenaline in us, which degenerates our organism. Positive attitude secretes endorphin in us, which regenerates our organism.

Recovering fundamental belief gives us, right away, a more positive attitude toward life. Then we've to improve further, both consciously and unconsciously.

For the conscious adjustments, we have an easy way out. Let's remember:

- We see outside what's inside us,

- We treat others the way we treat ourselves.

Hence, we start by having a more favorable look toward us; and by treating ourselves gentler. Then, all our conscious adjustments, with the immediate surrounding and with the external world, will be done automatically.

But, the process of adjusting attitude is progressive. Start with the easy steps.

Don't ruminate on how to do it; just do it. You learn while doing, you evolve while doing. As long as you remain aware of this evolution, your willpower will be reinforced, and the subsequent stages of your adjustment will become easier.

For example, Patrick decides his first step will be:

'Stop anger toward yourself.'

This eliminates his glasses of anger. Consequently, he sees less anger outside, radiates less anger toward others, and responds to others' anger with indifference. His perceptions, actions, and reactions become gentler.

His second step becomes:

'Stop doing injustice to yourself'.

His glasses of injustice drop. He sees less injustice outside, does less injustice to others, and responds to others' injustice with fairness.

As his attitude toward himself softens, he puts on his glasses of empathy.

He has more compassion toward himself. He sees compassion outside, acts with compassion toward others, and reciprocates others' compassion with more compassion.

The virtuous cycle of his recovery sets in.

On average, my clients need four to five steps to soften their attitude. And the average time required is two and a half months. The process, however, accelerates with your recovery:

More positive you become, quicker comes your future positivism.

All my clients begin with a long list of change.

But, as they progress in gentleness, they develop a lot more confidence in themselves. They accept a part of their frailty as the other face of their quality. This heightens their self-esteem.

They respect themselves more, they trust their instincts more, and their list of change shortens.

Their desire to control the uncontrollable disappears. Instead, they focus on their core task; their performance increases. As their cycle of recovery reinforces itself, they carry out the further changes effortlessly.

The conscious adjustments then seep into their unconscious.

If your terrain has lived under strain for too long, you also need to make adjustments to your unconscious.

That sounds contradictory:

How can you make conscious adjustments to your unconscious?

You can. Let's see how.

For example, an act of violence we commit today, or a thought of violence we let enter our mind now, will continue to affect our unconscious for weeks, even for months afterward. And, if we keep repeating such acts or thoughts, our unconscious will lean toward violence slowly, until we turn into violent individuals.

On the other hand, if we keep thinking gentle thoughts, and keep performing gentle actions, in a few months we become gentler.

The transformation happens within the alchemy of our being.

Thoughts and actions raise waves in our *ether*. The waves of violence differ from those of compassion; they impact our Individual Self, and transform it, differently. Our character changes, our biochemistry changes. These transformations then show upon us, as violent or compassionate individuals.

We become what we think, we become what we do.

At a riverside camp, outside a tent, a kayak and a pile of books attract my curiosity.

I take a closer look at the books—they are on neuroscience and theology. A woman crawls out of the tent.

"You like my books?"

"Why do you read theology?"

"Because…" She stands. "I am a doctor in neuroscience."

"Pardon me?"

"You don't see the connection?" She sighs. "Nobody does."

"I'll listen, if you explain."

"All these years, I'm trying to understand why my patients need a role model." Her head tilts backward. "Why our ancestors used one called 'God'?"

"What did you find?"

"God was created by Man." She picks up a book from the pile, and ruffles through it. "God represents the deepest desires of Man."

She holds the book up, with both hands. "See the European gods?" Flip. "The African gods?" Flip. "The Asian gods?" Flip…

"What should I see?"

"Look at their faces, their eyes." Her jaws stiffen. "What do you see in common?"

I take the book from her, and flip through the pages. "They all look gentle and serene."

"Then you see my point."

"No, I don't."

"Why do you think we created those images?" She crosses her arms over the belly. "Why do we need that image of serenity and gentleness before us?"

I scratch my head.

"Take a closer look at those devotees at the feet of gods."

Sharp pain distorts their faces. Their agitation stands in stark contrast with the poise of the gods.

I close the book. "We created those images to appease our inner turbulence."

She places her hands on the hips. "Now it's me who doesn't understand you."

"By visualizing those gods, we hope to become like them."

"Ah." Her hands come down. "You understand my patients then."

"I don't know your patients."

"I work with ex-convicts." She takes the book from me, and stacks it on her pile. "Those who want to change, seek out a role model."

"Serene and gentle?"

"Just the opposite of what they've been."

"Why do they choose God?"

"They don't." She frowns. "Those are for *me* only."

"Who do they choose?"

"A loving family member."

"And then?"

"I work with them, until that person's image is fixed on their mind."

"You help them replace their violent image with a gentle one."

She nods. "Then they feel serene. With themselves, and with others around them."

"You think there is a biochemical process behind their evolution?"

"Now you've hit the nail right on its head. But,"—she taps her foot—"you're entering a serious controversy between neuroscience and theology."

"It's *your* opinion that interests me."

"The stuff is commonsense." Her foot slips out of the sandal. "Gentleness and violence don't have the same effect on our neurotransmitters."

"Gentleness and violence don't have the same effect on our hormones either."

"Over the long term,"—she digs the soil with her toe—"those hormones and neurotransmitters alter the images in our memory."

"How do the traits of your patients change, when they transform?"

"Like what?" Her foot goes back into the sandal.

"Their looks, for example."

"They start with a dark aura. But, as gentleness takes over them,"—she paces back and forth—"a warm glow kindles their eyes. And the contours of their body soften."

"Does their body odor change too?"

"Yes." She stops. "I never thought along these lines, but it seems logical."

"Why?"

"When they evolve, the chemistry of their blood evolves too."

"All these begin with a serene and gentle image?"

She nods. "You need something concrete to work with."

"Like, someone in the family?"

"Or, someone outside, who has given them compassion."

"What if they never had someone gentle in the family? What if they never had a family at all? What if nobody ever gave them compassion?"

Her face twitches. "In that case, I make them visualize themselves. The way they used to be, before they became violent."

"That works?"

"Always."

"How?"

"Nobody is ever born violent, right?"

Nobody is born strained either.

Look for an image of yourself, before strain invaded your terrain. Then, visualize your thoughts and actions repeatedly, associated with that image. Soon it will anchor within your self, become your own model, and transform you from within.

186

Your hormones will change, your neurotransmitters will change, your digestion will change, your metabolism will change, your circulation will change, your muscles and joints will change, and your posture will change.

You'll change.

To accelerate your transformation, repeat positive words like 'robust', 'resilient', 'diligent, 'patient', and 'confident'. These words resonate within our body cavities that contain endocrine glands and nerve plexuses. The vibrations regenerate them, improve their functions.

You reinforce your transformation.

Regenerate your terrain

Our terrain has its elasticity, and a rhythm of its own. Under strain, it loses those, and jams passage of everything through it.

Moreover, a strained terrain has little autonomy, and degenerates rapidly.

To restore, we've to counteract the degenerative forces brought upon us by strain. These forces push us toward:

- Repression of emotions,

- Compulsive eating,

- Poor work habits,

- And little exercise.

By aligning accordance, we do arrest the degeneration of our terrain further, but then we've to release the repressed emotions, and sanitize our life-style. This needs effort.

The key to optimal recovery is: *doing just the right amount of fixing.*

Never overdo.

Depending upon the extent of strain, you may have to work with appropriate professionals. Nevertheless, the following guidelines will help you.

The inverted postures and the breathing protocols of yoga normalize pressure inside our body cavities, enhance neural impulses and blood flow to our organs, improve the ratio of oxygen to carbon-dioxide in our blood, and eliminate toxins better.

To strengthen heart and lungs, we need cardio-respiratory sports, in open air. A minimum of 30 to 40 minutes daily, at an optimal pulse rate, is required. We don't have to set aside extra time for this. A fast walk to our work will suffice.

What is the optimal pulse rate for cardio-respiratory sports?
It is 130%-150% of our resting pulse rate, which varies within a limit.

Here is how you calculate that rate:

1. On three different days, let's say your resting pulses are 52, 60, and 68.
2. The average: $(52 + 60 + 68)/3 = 60$
3. The lower range: $60 \times 130\% = 78$
4. The upper range: $60 \times 150\% = 90$

As your cardio-respiratory health improves, your resting pulse rate will drop. Every two or three months, recalculate your optimal pulse rate, and adjust the intensity of your sports.

Strain causes strange food habits—eating abnormal quantities, addiction to specific tastes, to name a few. Don't switch over to fanatic nutritional regimes; they'll do you more harm than good.

Eat everything that's nutritious and naturally tasty, but in small quantities.

And always leave one fourth of your stomach empty.

When strain is too chronic, use the following rules of thumb:

- If Air dominates your constitution, give preference to sweet, sour, and salty tastes. The post digestive energy of your aliments should be warm.

- If Bile dominates your constitution, give preference to sweet, bitter, and astringent tastes. The post digestive energy of your aliments should be cool.

- If Catarrh dominates your constitution, give preference to pungent, bitter, and astringent tastes. The post digestive energy of your aliments should be hot.

Why should a constitutional type give preference to certain tastes?
Within each cell of our body, there are two digestive *fires*.

In the membrane of our cell, the *fire* of microcellular digestion separates the *five elements* of nutrients ingested into the cell, and assimilates them with its *five elements*. Thus, *water* and *earth* from sweets reinforce the same constitutional elements of a cell, as well as they counteract its *air* and *ether*.

The *five elements* from nutrients also nourish our five senses.

Ether nourishes sound, *air* nourishes touch, *fire* nourishes vision, *water* nourishes taste, and *earth* nourishes smell.

When an Air-type's *ether* and *air* aggravate under strain, he suffers from auditory disturbances and dry skin; and, if his *water* and *earth* weaken, his appetite and smell suffer.

When he consumes aliments of sweet taste in moderation, *water* and *earth* from them replenish the same of his cells, and curb his excess *ether* and *air*.

His senses restore.

In the nucleus of our cell, the *fire* of microcellular consciousness assimilates the three qualities of food—balance, inertia, and motion—into the consciousness of our cell, then into the qualities of our mind.

For example, sweet taste is rich in inertia.

A moderate consumption of sweet aliments will calm the hyperactivity of an Air-type individual, whereas excess consumption of those aliments will make him lethargic.

Why should a constitutional type pay attention to the post-digestive energy of foods?

190

Let's consider a Bile-type personality.

Bile produces heat. Under strain, bile increases in him more than in others; so his organism heats up more than others too.

To cool this heat, he needs food with cold post-digestive energy.

What is post-digestive energy?

It's the energy that an aliment releases *after* digestion. A few examples will illustrate:

- Most sweets release cool energy after digestion, but not honey.
- Ice-cream and yogurt cool our body immediately, but heat it later.
- Black pepper heats us immediately, but cools us later.

As always, moderation is the best way out.

Moderate consumption of sweet aliments will cool the heat of the Bile-type, whereas excess consumption will clog his organism with hot mucus.

What to do without a professional?

Choosing aliments based on their post-digestive energy is tricky.

There are some charts, but your best guide is *your* organism.

So, experiment.

Taste a food; see how you feel a couple of hours later.

And stick to those foods that go with you.

How to eliminate stagnant emotions?

Discordance with self generates conflictual thoughts and emotions. Our organism evacuates them at several levels.

First, a few conflicts resolve consciously.

The rest gets shoved into our unconscious, a fraction of which escape via dreams. The remains creep along our nerves, seep into our terrain. There, in the cells, the *fire* of cellular consciousness digests them, normally.

But, not always.

Under strain, bombardment of conflicts exceeds all capacities of evacuation.

The unresolved conflicts stagnate in the *ether* of our intercellular spaces. This rigidifies our terrain, and destroys its elasticity and natural rhythm.

Our perceptions, actions, and reactions deviate from their optimal.

How these stagnant emotions affect us depends on our constitutional type:

    - For Air-type, the large intestine and the lungs lose their elasticity and rhythm

    - For Bile-type, the stomach and small intestines lose their elasticity and rhythm

    - For Catarrh-type, the heart and lungs lose their elasticity and rhythm

And, on the emotions we repress:

- From fear, our kidneys and reproductive organs lose their tonicity
- From anger, our liver and gall bladder lose their tonicity
- From jealousy, our heart and spleen lose their tonicity

The awareness exercise from chapter 2—neutralize emotions, by observing them—prevents new emotions from stagnating in our terrain, but doesn't evacuate those that are already there in the intercellular spaces. How do we empty them?

Let's return to our alchemy of *five elements*.

Thoughts propagate through our *ether* as waves. Once accordance with self has been established, the new thoughts come free of conflicts. The waves of these thoughts propagate through our terrain harmoniously, and start the repair work, but they can't always enter the deepest pockets of our organism where the stagnation hides.

We need a device that stirs and churns those stagnant emotions, and expels them from our intercellular spaces. Then only the waves of fresh concordant thoughts can penetrate into those spaces, and restore the tone and rhythm of our terrain.

What to do then?

Waves propagate by vibrations. To ensure deep penetration into our intercellular spaces, we need to enhance the vibrations of our harmonious thoughts. In the East, people use specific sounds to do that enhancement.

For example, in India people use 'AUM'.

'AUM' consists of three prolonged vowels that resonate in our cavities: 'A' vibrates inside the pelvic and the abdominal; 'U', inside the thoracic; and 'M', inside the cranial.

When we project 'AUM' from pelvis, potent resonances spread inside us from these cavities. Within twelve repetitions, we feel stagnations leaving our organism.

Do we have to use AUM always?
No.

'Good Morning', 'Bon Jour', 'Buenos Dias', or their equivalent in your language will do.

All these greetings have pitches similar to AUM. And they vibrate the same way inside us as AUM.

Pronounce these greetings sincerely, projecting your natural voice from the pelvis.

You can practice them on others, but avoid resenting them if they don't reciprocate. The benefits of these greetings come to you first, before they go to others.

Over long term, watch what these simple sounds do to your self-esteem.

To sustain your progress, you've to give *full* rest to your organism, regularly. Sleep is not enough for that.

During sleep, our mind moves through dreams; we feel agitated. To give complete rest to our organism, we need to approach it via its first element: *ether*, the emptiness. That is done by visualizing the infinity.

Tiffany, 37 years old, insurance professional, does it this way:

"When I close my eyes, I see the space." Her eyeballs roll under the lids.

"What's in there?"

"Planets and stars and…" Her eyeballs stop rolling. "A lot of emptiness. And I'm floating among them, all free."

In a few seconds, her eyes open. "I became part of that space."

"Did that scare you?"

"At first, yes. But then, I felt renewed."

Visualizing infinity stops all stimuli to the cerebrum—the part of our brain that analyses, judges, and thinks. The electrical charge of its neurons diminishes.

Subsequently, the cerebrum releases its grip on mid and lower brain—the parts that restore our organism after stress, and run it under balance. Our organism replenishes its reserves.

We feel refreshed.

Be reasonable with yourself

Rebuilding well-being requires patience and tolerance.

The minimum time I've seen is about two and a half months, but you don't have to wait that long to see results. Some benefits you see right away, the moment you recover your fundamental belief; the rest comes in steps. Others can encourage you in your recovery, but the true encouragement comes from inside you, when you see your evolution.

Your improvement becomes evident through the reduction of intensity and frequency of your symptoms. Most report 15%-20% progress per month.

The key to steady recovery is regularity.

When you do your tasks regularly, with awareness of your evolution, you don't fall into monotony. The same exercise shows you something different about you each time; and the same path reveals something different about the world, each time you walk upon.

Leave a margin for errors and setbacks.

Don't get caught into regrets and resentments, if you fail once in a while. Then you learn from your errors; the failures bring the teacher inside you out; you get up stronger, and run better.

All obstacles to your recovery don't depend upon you.

To avoid frustration, engage in a real passion—one that is not sold to you by others, but one that originates from within you.

When you engage in such a passion, your destructive energy turns constructive. You do your best on what's within your power; the rest you leave out, with a smile.

Where do we find such passion?
Look in your childhood.

196

Three out of four trace their passion before ten.

What if your original solution clashes with other trainings you received?

It will, inevitably. Christian, 37 years old, account manager, reconciles these clashes as follows.

"At first, I was lost." He shakes his head. "The conflict management and influencing strategies I learnt from our trainer baffled me completely."

"Why?"

"I wouldn't motivate myself, nor manage my own conflicts, that way."

"What was your training for?"

"To work better with my colleagues." He slaps his knee. "But, not for me."

"What do you mean?"

"I was in a critical period of my life." He raises his hand. "I absolutely needed to manage my own conflicts first, to motivate myself at work." He smacks his lips. "Naturally, in their repertoire of strategies, I searched for one that would work for me."

"And you didn't find one."

"Now I know why."

"Tell me what you did."

He pulls a sheet of paper and draws three rectangles.

"First, I laid my personal strategy, inside out, in the three spheres, as you asked." He slides the sheet toward me. "Then I placed their strategies next to mine."

"And you saw they fit together."

He raises his thumb. "I even grasped their strategy a lot better, in the light of my own."

What if my original solution bruises my old wounds?
They always do. But Loren, 53 years old, writer, transforms those bruises into arts.

"These wounds, these sores from the past,"—she swallows—"they serve me in my work."

"You create from them."

She nods. "But, they hurt."

"How do you go around?"

"You don't, Monsieur Garai." She snaps her fingers. "Instead, you dig into those wounds, and fetch your riches from their depth."

"You ignore the pain in the process?"

"No, I accept that pain as a part of the whole."

"What happens to the wound?"

"It heals."

"Your sorrow transforms into joy then."

"These are the only joys that last, Monsieur Garai." She touches her chest. "And nourish us from inside."

Once your original solution pulls you out of strain, you've to prevent its recurrence by living wholesome.

Let's see what 'wholesome living' is.

13: By maintaining our well-being with wholesome living

What is wholesome living?

A wholesome life:

> -Embraces the whole,
>
> -Renews itself,
>
> -Runs smoothly.

There is only *one* life-style that allows us to meet these three criteria: one that grows from within us, in accordance with our self, and in synergy with the rest.

That is our wholesome living.

A wholesome life envelops all, sustains by itself, and eliminates all our conflicts—with ourselves, our immediate surrounding, and our external world.

"I don't believe those speculative philosophies," says Virginia, 32 years old, human resources consultant. "But, feeling part of something larger, assures me."

"Are you referring to God?"

"I don't know if God exists." Her shoulders rise and fall. "All I believe is what I see."

"What do you see?"

"Small and big things in our life—all fall in their places, when we do our part right. These can't be simple coincidences,

Monsieur Garai. We're not isolated entities floating around, with no links to others around us."

"How does that philosophy help you?"

"Have you ever been a control freak?" Her forehead creases. "I'm sure you have. You know then how much it burns."

"When?"

She blows. "When you can't control everything."

"What changes with your belief?"

"You know some things will resolve by themselves."

"Then, why do people control everything?"

"I can't speak for others." She straightens the pleats of her skirt. "I do it when I'm feeling vulnerable. When I don't want anything to go out of my hands, and hurt me."

Her 'something larger' is our Universal Self.

Within it, every Individual Self should proceed along its unique course proactively, in full autonomy, but in harmony with the rest.

That's wholesome living.

What unwholesome living brings for us

Three issues:

-We feel lonely everywhere; fear looms over us. We ask, 'Why am I here, all alone?'

-We stagnate in life; boredom invades us. We ask, 'Why do I rot in my ruts?'

-We have friction with everyone, including ourselves; conflicts devour us. We ask, 'Why do I always run with squeaks?'

Our terrain loses its elasticity and rhythm.

Our attitude hardens. Smallest jerks throw us out of our equilibrium.

Of those, who don't feel well but can't give a concrete definition of their unwell-being, 98% quote at least one of the three existential issues above. They complain of 'living in limbo'. The exchange below depicts this feeling in concrete terms:

"What is an average man composed of today, Monsieur Garai?" says Virginia.

"Air, ether, fire—"

"Stop!" She swerves her head. "Stop feeding me that bullshit of yours."

"Okay. What is an average man composed of today, Virginia?"

"Void." She stretches her arms out. "An enormous void."

"That's *ether*."

"Please!" She bends over my desk. "You know the kind of void I'm talking about: ISOLATION."

"Where do you see that?"

"Everywhere. People fidgeting in their corners—their ears covered, their eyes lowered, their fingers clattering on phones, their faces radiating suspicion…"

"Suspicion? Of what?"

"Of everyone. Of everything." Her bangs sway across her forehead. "And then they whine: 'Save me! Save me! I'm depressed.'"

I wipe my face. "That's *all* that people have today?"

"No. They have their bags of repressions, tons of gadgets, and mountains of boredom."

"Come on, Virginia. Do you really believe people are that miserable?"

"Do I believe it?" She leans forward. "Look at what I do. Get up, take the metro with a bunch of grumps, then work with them, lunch with them, chat with them—"

"Alright, alright. But you do escape them in vacations."

"Escape them? In vacations? When you take the same train with them to the beach? And then lie fifty centimeters away from them?" She grunts. "Pure ruts, Monsieur Garai. Life just stinks."

"Virginia." I raise my hand. "Those people certainly don't like challenges. Why don't you engage in challenging activities during vacations?"

She taps her foot. "That won't break my routine here."

"Why not introduce challenges here?"

"How, Monsieur Garai?" Her chin juts. "In our obsession with safety and security,"—she swipes her hand over my desk—"we've filtered all challenges out of our lives."

"There is no problem then."

"Right. That's why we invent problems." Her eyes narrow. "Then we analyze them for ten years, until they become real." She blows. "I get so fed up with my friends."

"What do they do?"

"They complain, Monsieur Garai. Nonstop. And do all those stupid things, just to shake off their loneliness."

"Like what?"

"Wear the latest fashion, go to the trendiest places, try the latest craze… anything, just to draw attention. And then what? " Her head tilts backward. "Monotony doesn't buy company."

"Company won't fill that void inside."

"Exactly." She grimaces. "That's why I yell at them: 'Stop complaining! If you want to go somewhere in life, shut your mouth, and do something.'"

"And they listen?"

"Are you kidding?" She sways her index. "You can't change a person, Monsieur Garai. The change has to come from inside."

How wholesome living makes us unique

We're never exactly like our father or mother. At the moment of conception, the Universe introduces a new element inside us. It's this element that gives us the potential to become unique.

To realize this potential, the Universe also sets forth a unique course for our evolution.

Along that course, however, *we* have to make our own destiny, by *our* proactive thoughts and actions. If we are to realize our uniqueness, these thoughts and actions better be in line with our fundamental belief, and in synergy with the rest.

That's where wholesome living comes in.

A wholesome life stays dynamic and intense. We embrace our actions and emotions of each instant; all ruts stay out of our life. Whatever we think or do, we remain aware of our evolution; all stagnations stay away from us. Neither our body nor our mind ages prematurely.

A wholesome life stays free of regrets and resentments. Everything that occurs in our life has a meaning: it contributes to our evolution. All that 'should have' or 'could have' happened are meaningless illusions.

Wholesome living lifts us to our utmost efficiency and effectiveness. We channel our energy into what we're best at; the rest, we leave to the Universal Self.

We reach our inherent potential, and become unique.

In practical terms, how do we live wholesome?
Let's go inside-out:

       -from within us,

       -to our immediate surrounding,

       - to our external world.

{Within us}

Within the sphere of 'us', let's see how we can live wholesome with respect to our body, mind, and Individual Self.

Body

How can we embrace our body, renew it, and avoid friction with it?
For an active person of good health, this boils down to wholesome nutrition, regular exercise, and a few rules of basic life-style hygiene.

Wholesome nutrition
Eat balanced meals that embrace all essential nutrients and all six tastes.

Avoid processed food altogether. Prepare your meals from primary matters that are naturally tasty, have natural fibers, and release energy progressively. Vary the ingredients of your meals, through weeks and through seasons.

Why should our meals embrace all six tastes?
A specific part of our tongue picks up a specific taste, and relays it to a part of our brain. Our brain then uses it to stimulate a part of our terrain. If we eat one taste in repetition, we stimulate only a part of our terrain. This pushes our body and mind out of equilibrium.

Let your tongue guide you. Your tongue knows when to push you toward a little sugar or a little pepper. Don't fight with your tongue, unless it pushes you toward excess.

Never eliminate any taste completely; never eat all hot or all cold foods.

Eat all, but in small quantities.

Excess kills us more than hunger. Eat food, but don't let food eat you.

Fill half of your stomach with solid food, one-fourth with liquid, and leave the rest empty for passage of aliments, oxygen, and excrements.

Eat with awareness. Feel what different tastes do to your mouth, to your body, mind, and spirit.

Stress cuts the movements of our intestines; cut stress out of your diet. Leave all analysis, planning, and conflicts out of your meals. Switch off the TV, the phones, and all else that distract you from your food.

Our digestive organs need rest.

Leave at least five hours between meals. Drink nothing but plain water in those spaces.

One day per week, skip breakfast and lunch. Avoid hard physical and mental works on that day. Drink two to three liters of plain water during that period. These regular fasts do a lot for our organism.

During the first five-six hours, our liver cleans the blood. A minor headache may occur during this period, as well as some palpitation and vertigos, if our organism is not used to low blood sugar.

In the next three to four hours, the fast works on our neurotransmitters. We may feel a little 'drunk', but our consciousness and senses sharpen later.

Beyond these hours, the fast works on our unconscious. Stagnant emotions leave intercellular spaces, our internal tensions release, and the awareness of our Individual Self deepens.

Keep your colon free from all congestions. In chronic constipation, nine out ten find the following recipe efficient.

Mix five tablespoons of whole grain cereals with two teaspoons of wheat germ, one-fourth teaspoons of cumin and coriander seeds, and four to five black cardamoms peeled. Roast them lightly, in a pan without oil. Add a pinch of salt, and take the mix as breakfast with natural yogurt. Add a few dates and figs if you like.

The mix above also regenerates the muscular walls of your colon.

Eat whole grains, cereals, fruits, and vegetables with skin. Never mix fish or meat with dairy products. Don't overuse dietary fibers or commercial laxatives; they inflame your colon and degenerate it over the long term.

Depending on your weight, drink one to two litters of plain water per day. If your colon doesn't flush spontaneously in the morning, use the following technique.

Before you go to sleep, fill a copper bowl with lukewarm water, squeeze one-fourth of lime in it, add a pinch of salt, and leave the mix overnight. When you wake up, drink this mix, and then squat on the floor and breathe deeply.

The movements of the diaphragm will massage your colon against the pressure from the thighs; within fifteen minutes, your colon will start to move.

If toxins have lodged inside your colon, you may see loose stools toward the end of evacuation. If this happens, boil a green apple and a green banana, mash them together, add a pinch of salt, turmeric, and black pepper; and then start your dinner with this mix.

This astringent mix absorbs the toxins from your colon, and evacuates them with your stool next morning.

Keep your tongue lean and clean. If you see a thick coat, yellow or white, that's because catarrh has deposited on your organs. Clean your tongue with a spoon twice per day, and use the following mix.

In a tablespoon of honey, add a pinch of basilica, ginger, pepper, and cinnamon powders. Mix them into a paste, and then absorb it under your tongue, fifteen minutes before breakfast.

Avoid incompatible mixes of foods. Establish your list through trial and error, and then stick to your list. Do not let others wheel you into extreme dietary regimes; they do more harm than the incompatible mixes.

Control your diet, but don't let your diet control you.

Exercise and other life-style hygiene:

Our exercise program should encompass all the functional units within the body.

Vary your mix of exercises, and perform them regularly. Whatever you choose must not weigh upon you.

Avoid cardio-respiratory training in closed places. They put unnecessary strain on our lungs and heart.

Depending on your constitutional type, use the following rule of thumb:

- If Air-type dominates your constitution, avoid exhaustion on windy days,
- If Bile-type dominates, avoid exhaustion on hot days,
- If Catarrh-type dominates, avoid exhaustion on humid days.

Avoid stooping postures altogether.

They degenerate our vertebral column, diminish neural impulses to our organs, impede the movements of our diaphragm, and reduce oxygen and blood supply to the brain. Our physical and psychological functions, as well as our mood suffer.

To maintain your posture erect, always keep your tail bone and chin tucked in slightly. Strengthen the muscles around your vertebral column, by forward bend, backward bend, twist, and inclination to both sides. If you choose the route of yoga, 'pada-hastasana', 'bhujangasana', 'ardha-matsyendrasana', and 'ardha-chandrasana' will suffice.

If you can, do three series of 'kapalbhati' and 'nauli' in fresh air, before breakfast. They decongest our visceral organs, improve their tonicity, and clean our sinuses.

We've already seen what 'sarvangasana' does for us.

Exercise with awareness, of your movement and your breathing. Feel how your body and mind react to the exercise; which new aspect of you is revealed in the process. Don't look at the watch; let your body tell you when to stop.

Change the context of your exercise regularly. Push yourself beyond your limits at times, and watch how your robustness and resilience increase.

Leave a margin for errors, and room for surprises.

In all exercises, avoid excess.

Do only those exercises that correspond to *you*. Maintain regularity, but also keep flexibility in your schedule. Don't feel guilty to take a day off, and float around.

While exercising, focus on happy thoughts. I asked 32 runners to do this during their training. Their endurance increased by an average of 21%.

Positive attitude secretes endorphins, the natural pain killers. Our tolerance of pain increases, and we don't feel the pain of training.

Also, these endorphins, secreted naturally, remain longer in our blood than the artificial ones. Our mood stays elevated for many hours, after the exercise session has finished.

Moreover, these natural endorphins never tax our body or mind.

Always keep your exercises simple; they go better with our self.

Mind

We can embrace the conscious part of our mind, renew it, and avoid frictions with it. But, how do we embrace our unconscious?

We do that by allowing our intuition to take over our logic at times.

"It's true, when I sit down to write, I follow a structure," says Evelyn, professor and writer. "But, within that structure, I let my mind run free."

"What does that mean?"

"I let my thoughts pour onto the screen." Her fingers drum on my desk. "Then I look at them. And figure out what my unconscious is trying to tell me."

"That doesn't ruin your structure?"

"No."

"Do you see coherence among your thoughts?"

"Yes." She adjusts the glasses on the bridge of her nose. "Sometimes, they may look like isolated icebergs, but I know something connects them underneath."

"What?"

"The ocean of my unconscious."

"What would happen if you reasoned with them from the beginning?"

"They'll sink deeper. I'll never see them again."

"Why do you call them icebergs?"

"Their largest parts hide under my consciousness." She touches the base of her throat. "I've to plunge deep, and push them up to the surface."

"Do they clash?"

"I knew you would ask that question." She turns toward me. "No, they rarely do."

"Why?"

"My unconscious had seen their coherence with the whole already."

Our unconscious never dissociates from the consciousness. Nevertheless, we can still do something to integrate them better.

Feeling the digital pulses reduces the bombardments from the upper brain toward the lower brain. This relieves our unconscious, regenerates it, and aligns it better with our consciousness.

Balancing on one foot strengthens the opposite side of the brain. The two halves integrate more efficiently; we achieve a better balance between our creativity and analytics. The inverted postures of yoga, and those that imitate reptiles, stimulate our lower brain centers, and strengthen our unconscious.

We achieve a more effective coherence across the entire spectrum of our mind.

What impedes the renewal of our mind?

Excess security.

Trade it for freedom.

"Jack London's Buck didn't just eat, sleep, and walk," says Nicolas, 46 years old, chief editor of a major publishing house. "Buck left the sun of the southland, to join a pack of wolves in the cold."

"Well, Buck didn't have a choice exactly. He was hitched out of his home, to drag a sledge across the arctic."

He nods. "Jack London, himself, didn't doze in an armchair either. Why do you think he put Buck through that enormous challenge?"

"For him, Buck had potential. But, he had reached his limits at home."

"Right." He stands up and walks to the window. "So, he killed Buck's mediocre existence in one shot, and sent him on that perilous trail." He turns around and leans against the glass pane. "Do you think Buck had the qualities to survive those perils?"

"Yes, but they were sleeping inside him. They woke up when the dangers surrounded him, all at once."

He sits on the ledge. "Did he learn new skills on the road?"

"Yes. How to lead a pack of dogs on the snow, and—"

He slaps the sill. "And then Buck reached his limits again. What did he do?"

"He responded to the call from within. He left the pack of dogs, to lead a pack of wolves in the wild."

"Buck was impulsive for sure." He strides back to his seat. "But, was he rash in his decisions?"

"No. He let his instincts guide him. That's why, over that frozen river, he refused to drag the sledge. He accepted the thrashing from his owner instead."

"What happened next?"

"When the glacier collapsed under the weight of the sledge, the rest of the pack drowned in a crevasse, along with their owner."

He touches my forearm. "Who was Buck?"

"A creature from London's unconscious."

Unknown situations offer us opportunities for fresh learning.

When we judge these situations solely by our conscious logic, fear grips us; we turn these opportunities down. We close ourselves from new experiences. We stagnate.

On the contrary, when we embrace these opportunities, we force our intuition to work in the face of risks. And then, when we observe our perceptions, actions, and reactions in these situations, we see our evolution. We break out of our limits.

These fresh experiences then seep into our unconscious, renew our experiential base, and prepare us for the future risks, equipped with a larger set of competences. Our fear is replaced by courage.

Trust your instincts. They'll never push you too far out of your limits, nor too quickly. In the face of a challenge, you may think you're taking illogical risks, but your unconscious acts behind you—to calculate the risks of your moves, and then to match them against your renewed capacities.

When we trust our instincts, they bring the best inside us out, and take us where we're meant to go.

Security and insecurity—both become illusions for us.

One spring, in a small village, my train is cancelled.

On the platform across, a woman howls on her mobile phone. On the road before her, a little boy picks up things from the pavement, and then deposits them in a bush. I cross the tracks and walk toward them.

"Snails." The boy picks one up, and holds it under my eyes. "They're coming from that bush."

"What are you doing with them?"

"I'm taking them to their home." He darts to the bush, and puts the snail on a branch.

"Why do you worry? They can slide back by themselves."

"No!" He cringes. "The cars will crash them on their way."

"Oh, I see."

I join him in his endeavor.

A few minutes later, a group of hikers march onto the platform, and disperse a flight of sparrows chattering under the sun. The next train is an hour and a half later. The hikers gather under the announcement board and start complaining bitterly.

One hiker, tired of neighing and whining, approaches us. We explain our action, and she joins us.

Next minute, another hiker joins us. And then another…

Soon the entire group, including the kid's mother, move imprudent snails off the road to the bush.

Their fitful laughter lifts the cloud of impatience over the station.

We are *all* born with a flexible mind. Later, prejudice and habits rigidify it. Once we pluck these leeches off, our mind recovers its elasticity; and our senses, their vitality.

We become capable again, to learn from what surrounds us.

How do we prevent frictions with our mind?

External conflicts we can avoid, resolve, or manage. But, when it comes to internal conflicts, there is only one viable option: resolve. Whatever internal conflict, major or minor, we don't resolve will grate within us nonstop.

Fortunately, we can resolve all our internal conflicts with one simple strategy:

Act the way it feels right, no matter how inconvenient the consequences are.

When we adhere to this, our mind never squeaks.

Whenever we compromise, no matter to what degree, guilt grinds us from inside.

Guilt poses serious threats to our mind, by pushing us slowly toward explosion. Let's understand this through an analogy.

Think of a gas cylinder. Inside it, gas stays compressed against hard metal. If a flame enters the cylinder, the gas ignites, the pressure increases exponentially, until the metal walls can't resist anymore, and the cylinder explodes.

Guilt scrapes our conscience nonstop. We can escape all, but never our own conscience.

To withstand this continual torment, our conscience hardens. Our guilt then stays compressed within that rigid conscience. The smallest of conflicts ignite a flame within us, our internal pressure multiplies, and we explode.

At a milder level, guilt may not explode us immediately, but the hardened conscience increases our risk of being sandwiched between the stresses from inside and outside. Our threshold between stress and strain lowers, and our vulnerability rises.

A man free from internal conflicts stays free from internal pressure. Guilt never invades his mind, nor hardens his conscience; hence, the external pressure has nothing to sandwich his mind against. He has no risk for nervous breakdown.

A man, acting in accordance with his values, always remains free from internal conflicts. He either resolves a stressful situation, or rejects it altogether.

Individual Self

Next, let's see how we can embrace our individual self—that is, our atman— renew it, and avoid friction with it.

"How do I take care of my atman?" Ask Indra, the chief of gods, and Vicara, the chief of demons.

Unable to find the answer, they head toward the forest home of Prajapati, their father and teacher.

To please him, Vicara takes seven elephants around his waist, thirty huge sacks of grains on each shoulder, and three hundred sixty-five barrels of wine on his head. On the contrary, Indra brings only two of his best celestial beauties—one black like the night, and one white like the day.

They wait in front of Prajapati's gate, glaring at each other. Prajapati finishes his meditation and comes out.

"Why all those elephants?" Prajapati points to Vicara.

"For your travel, Father. One for each day of the week." Vicara loosens his arms, and the elephants thud to the ground, heaving a sigh of relief.

"Why did you carry them?"

"Father, they won't come otherwise." Vicara slaps their buttocks hard, and they scream in agony.

"Stop!" Prajapati catches Vicara's hand. "Remember, I can walk? Let them return to their place."

Immediately, the elephants trumpet and dash into the forest, trampling the bushes on their way.

"And all those sacks on your shoulders!" Prajapati sighs. "They could feed the whole world for a millennium."

"They too are for you, Father. One for lunch, and one for dinner." Vicara dumps the sacks at Prajapati's feet. "Now you'll never starve to death."

"No, I'll die under those sacks." Prajapati shakes his head.

Vicara smiles nervously. Indra beams on his beauties; they wink back, with their conch eyes.

"Alright, Father." Vicara heaves. And, with a slap of his right hand, he sends all the sixty sacks flying.

"And all that wine? Are they for me too?"

"Yes, Father. One barrel per day."

"Dump them, before they ruin this world."

"Done, Father." With a slap of his left hand, Vicara sends the three hundred sixty-five barrels flying.

"And you?" Prajapati turns to Indra. "You can't walk a step without leaning on your women?"

Indra's arms drop from around their waists. Vicara chuckles.

"For your pleasure, Father." Indra clears his throat. "One for the day, and one for the night."

"Are you out of your mind?" Prajapati sways his index. "They are my daughters!"

Vicara heehaws, shaking from head to feet.

"Sorry, Father." Indra looks askance. "I forgot."

"Let them return to their places." Prajapati shakes his head. "And never do this to me again."

221

Day flies into the day; Night, into the night.

"Now, you both." Prajapati crosses his arms over the chest. "What brings you here?"

"Father, we've expanded our territories as far as we could." Indra extends his arm toward north; Vicara, toward south. "There is nothing left for us to conquer, unless you allow us to fight." They grind their teeth at each other. "What do we do next?"

"Ah, the monotony. Time weighing on the spirit." Prajapati broods. "Have you taken care of your atman?"

"We don't know how to do that, Father." They stare at the ground. "That's why we've come here, to find out from you."

"Alright. Stay with me for thirty-two years."

On the first day of the thirty-third year, Prajapati takes them to a lake.

"What do you see?" Prajapati points to the still water.

"Us, Father. Our limbs, our hair, our eyes…"

"Now go back, dress in your best clothes, and return."

They do.

"What do you see now?"

"Us, Father. In our best clothes."

"That's your atman. Now, go home, and take care of it."

Vicara immediately returns to his territory and announces: 'Wanna take care of your atman? Then, dress in your best clothes!'

All demons do. At funerals, they dress the corpses in their best clothes, and put them on the pyre.

Indra, on his way back, sees the trap; he returns.

"What brings you back?" Prajapati asks.

"Father, clothes never touch our atman."

"So?"

"We can't take care of it by dressing in the best clothes. How do we do it then?"

"Live with me for another thirty-two years."

During these thirty-two years, Indra observes the frugal lifestyle of Prajapati. Indra, the perfectionist, of course, takes that regime to its extreme. At the end, Prajapati takes him back to the same lake.

"What do you see?"

"My bones, Father." Indra quakes at his image.

"That's your atman. Go now. Take care of it."

Again, on his way back, Indra sees the trap, and returns.

"Why are you back this time?" Prajapati says.

"Father, during those thirty-two years, I longed for food, wine, and pleasure. My atman cried all along with me."

"Live with me for another thirty-two years."

This time, Indra adopts the path of moderation.

"What do you see?" Prajapati asks by the lake.

"Me, Father. Just me. The way I am."

"Do you like what you see?"

"I think so." Indra rubs his forearm. "Yes, I do."

"You're coming close. Do you like what you do?"

"May be." Indra scratches his head. "Yes, I do."

"Take notes from now on." Prajapati hands him a stack of banana leaves, a peacock feather, and a pot of ink.

"Notes of what, Father?" Indra sighs at the stack.

"What you think, what you do."

"How?"

"Live with me for another five years."

Finally, at the end of one hundred and one years, Indra sits at Prajapati's feet.

Prajapati touches his head. "It's time for you to leave, Son."

Indra looks up. "We don't go to the lake anymore?"

"We don't need to."

Indra hands him the stack of banana leaves. "What do I do with these?"

"Those are your best friends." Prajapati pushes them back. "Keep them for life. Do you recall what you came here for?"

"To know how to take care of my atman."

"How do you?"

"By devoted work."

"Which work can you devote to?"

"One that corresponds to my atman."

"Where is your atman?"

"All over me."

"Do excesses help it?"

"No."

"Do austerities help it?"

"No."

"What helps it then?"

"Moderation."

"Why?"

"Moderation doesn't distract me from devoted work."

"What's next?"

"I don't care, Father. As long as I know I'm evolving." Indra lowers his eyes. "If I do my task at hand right, I know my atman will guide me to the next."

"Go back now. Continue working in that spirit."

"Father." Indra bites his lip. "What if I lose my work?"

"You'll still have its result."

"What if I lose that too?"

Prajapati crosses his arms over the chest. "What's your most valuable result?"

Indra scratches his head. "My evolution."

"Does that ever leave you?"

"No."

Let's proceed to our immediate surrounding now.

{Within our immediate surrounding}

Our immediate surrounding consists of colleagues, friends, and family.

At work

How do we embrace the whole?
By remaining modest.

"Businesses have meaning *only* during their times," says Helene, 56 years old, human resources manager. "Some we see today would have looked delirious a few years ago."

"Give me an example."

"These mobile phones." She takes hers out of the handbag and places it on my desk. "They didn't exist when I was a teenager. Nobody told us we needed them." Her fingers type on the keypad of the phone. "Today, we can't even go to the toilet without them."

"What does that mean?"

"These phones, and their makers—they rule our lives now. But, one day, both would disappear too."

"How?"

"Wait till someone invents a digital bomb that diffuses through these networks. Then this mobile business will shut down overnight."

"But, in the meantime, they—"

"They churn our economy." She beams. "People work for them. With their salaries, they buy bread, pay rents. With that rent, the landlord buys his meat. With the price of that meat, the butcher pays for his kids—"

Her phone buzzes. She presses a key without looking at it.

"Within a company, are the posts also temporary?"

"Sure. Posts are created, eliminated, then recreated."

"Can you give me an example?"

"Look at the world of finance. Those products they call 'derivatives'." The screen of her phone lights; she turns it over. "Until a couple of years ago, every bank died to have them. Today, every bank is dying to get rid of them."

"What happened to their creators?"

"Made millions first, and then went to jail."

"In absolute time, those jobs are not significant then?"

"No more than yours or mine."

Her phone vibrates. She switches it off, and shoves it into her handbag.

"You can answer that phone, Helene."

She flings her hand over the head. "All these jobs, they do only one thing: feed people, and their fantasies."

"What does that say about your job?"

"Stay modest."

All jobs serve only one purpose: to ensure the continuity of our society, in their time.

When we stay modest and do our best, we approach our inner self with dignity.

When we go around boasting about our jobs or comparing with others, we lose ourselves in the social mirrors.

How do we renew ourselves?
By remaining aware of our evolution.

Even the most repetitive tasks, if we do them with awareness of our evolution, they show us something new about us every time. We never stagnate in our place and rot.

"Each time I answer the phone, I learn something new about me and the caller," says Jamila, medical assistant at a clinic.

"Can you give an example?"

"Like, the tone of my voice decides the course of the caller's behavior."

"What do you do with that knowledge?"

"Grow my skills. I've been at this job for six years, but never been bored once."

We can also help our growth through the right training.

Discuss your evolutionary objectives with your manager, and then go through the appropriate training. If within your influence, make sure the entire department benefits from your initiative.

When that happens, everyone wins together.

How do we avoid conflicts?

"Conflicts don't have to become combats," says Brice, Chief Operating Officer of a multinational research company. "If we respect the rights and perspectives of others."

"When can we do that?"

"When we feel secure about ours." He straightens his tie. "Then we can penetrate into the skin of others, without feeling threatened by them."

"What do you do when someone attacks *you,* instead of the problem?"

"I don't attack back. I divert his energy into the problem." He leans forward. "Then, I show him what he is good at. That ends the conflict, most of the time."

"Do you expect him to do the same for you?"

"No. But, an argument won is a cause lost. Most know that."

"What do you do when your subordinates make mistakes?"

"If they recognize their mistakes, I let them save face. Then I let them handle their own mistakes. They learn in the process."

"You don't give them advice?"

"Only if they ask. They know I'm there, if they need me."

"How do you handle when someone above you thinks differently?"

"I listen first. Then I state my own perspective, firmly but politely."

"How?"

"To assert, you need two things." He raises his thumb and index. "One, to have a stance of your own." The thumb folds. "Two, to accept that your superior can have a stance different from yours." The index folds. "Then you can communicate your perspective, while respecting your superior's."

"Authority doesn't intimidate you?"

"Not if I stand ready to assume the consequences of my stance." He raises his palm. "We always have to have an alternative in life, Monsieur Garai. Without that, there is no respectful negotiation, nor freedom."

Conflicts are inevitable in *all* relations.

Two persons can *never* have exactly the same perspective on an issue. But, if they have dignity and empathy, they can turn their conflict into collaboration, by focusing on the complementarities of their perspectives.

Both win in that case.

Most of the time, one of the two has to rise above the conflict first, see the complementarities between the two, and then help the other see it. If you're secure within, you can be the person who takes that lead.

That security comes when you're living wholesome—in accordance with your self, and in synergy with the rest.

What if our job doesn't correspond to us?
Seven out of ten who say they don't like their job, end up liking it after retrieving accordance with self. Those who quit jobs without

aligning accordance, experience the same discontentment in their new jobs.

Others, however, genuinely need to change their jobs.

"All I do in my job is massaging numbers," says Jocelyn, a business strategy consultant.

"You don't like numbers?"

"I do, but not when I'm forced to manipulate them,"—her face turns to the side—"to produce documents that my clients would then use to enforce dirty company politics."

"Give me an example."

She tightens her belt. "In three banking assignments, my biggest clients used those documents to fire honest employees."

"I can see how that hurts your self esteem."

"Wait! You haven't heard the worst yet." Her lips stretch tight across her teeth. "In my last project, we developed the strategy for a pharmaceutical company, to expand into health foods."

"They must have hired new people."

"Big joke!" She shakes her head. "They used my analysis only to obtain financing from banks."

"Your work *did* serve something then."

"Right." She sniffles. "I wrote a sixty-page recommendation for this client." The corner of her mouth twists. "Their Chief Financial Officer just flipped through it, then ripped two pages from the financials, and excused himself to go to the bank."

Her eyes glisten. "Do you think I went to the business school to become a corporate pimp?"

Jocelyn ended up working for one of her clients. What they did for her, and what she did for them, corresponded more to her self.

With friends

How do we embrace and renew them?

One summer, I meet a group of volunteers in Kolkata.

All are executives, in late twenties to early thirties. They've taken the summer off, from their work and from the beaches, to sweat at Mother Teresa's center for abandoned children.

Two of them fall sick, and a woman from the group asks me for a reliable hospital.

"Why do you people take the pain to come here?" I ask.

Her shoulders stoop. "Pain isn't less elsewhere."

"Why do you say that?"

"Work, rant with friends, over the same old ruts, then eat, sleep, and go back to work…" Her nose crinkles. "Do you call that a life?"

"What's different here?"

"Here we make real friends," Her eyes glitter. "Around a real passion."

"What do you call real passion?"

233

"Real passion gives life." Her forehead furrows. "Here, we pull ourselves together, and think how to give life to these kids."

"But, how does that help *you*?"

"Come on!" She snaps her fingers. "These kids show us we can have a life too."

Real friendship embraces the Individual Self of friends. One plus one exceeds two.

Renew your friendships around challenges; they bring the best in people out.

Some drop out. Let them; they would have disappeared anyway, when challenges came.

Only those bonds, tied with durable values, endure.

How do we avoid friction with them?
Rules for avoiding frictions with friends parallel those with colleagues.

Whenever possible, act more and speak less. The benefits come to you first, before going to others.

"When I talk too much with my friends,"—Mirabelle slides her palm along the throat—"I don't feel well in the evenings."

"What happens?"

"Can't fall asleep, go to the toilette every hour, feel nervous and weak. Like I've emptied myself out. Why?"

"You just touched your throat. When you speak, what happens there?"

"My vocal chord vibrates."

"What's near the vocal chord?"

Her eyes fog. She pokes her throat with the index. Then she looks up at the anatomical chart over my desk.

"Ah, the thyroid." She startles. "When I speak, my vocal cord shakes my thyroid."

"What happens when it's shaken nonstop?"

"Goes crazy." The skin between her eyebrows creases. "And I become crazy too."

Continual blabber not only dilutes us before others but also drains our creativity; we lose authority, and end up non-distinct.

Keep your sacred garden secret.

And leave some space on your agenda, for yourself.

At home

How do we embrace all at home?

"Home binds people by love," says Veronique, Director of Research at an investment bank, and mother of two children. "Love sets very different objectives at home."

"Like what?"

"Grow together. Never at the expense of others."

"What quality do we require for that?"

"Personal sacrifice." She pulls her earlobe. "Each member sacrifices a bit, for the benefit of the whole."

"All come out winner at the end."

"Right." Her nose flares. "But some think spending time with children deprives them of opportunities."

"How do *you* see your time with your kids?"

"When my children learn something, their learning influences me." Her index uncoils a curl on her temple. "And the process works the other way too."

"What do you mean?"

She clears her throat. "Each child has an adult inside, waiting to come out." She scratches her cheek. "When we, the parents, learn something new, or do something new, that shows we, the adults, can still grow. And that influences our children."

"You grow your children by your growth."

"That's lot more effective than raising your finger at them."

"Why?"

"A relation of force destroys a relation of confidence."

She leans forward. "Children, especially before twelve, model after their parents." Her knuckles tap the edge of my desk. "If they hold us in high esteem, they do that even more."

"When you sacrifice for them, you rise higher in their esteem."

"Absolutely." She sits upright. "They observe more than they listen. They do what *we* do, with inspiration. They become what *we* think of them."

The *ether* of our intimates connects intimately.

Thoughts permeate within a family more than we think.

"My daughter's restlessness worried me," says Carmen, stewardess of a European airliner. "She wanted to go to a seaside camp."

"Did she?"

"No, I didn't let her." She clutches her kneecaps. "I was afraid of her security. So, we stopped talking about it altogether."

"Did her restlessness start after that?"

"Well… First, she started having problems at school." Her thumb slides along a pleat of the skirt. "Then, a pediatrician opened my eyes."

"Finally, you let your daughter go."

She shakes her head. "In my hotel room, I weighed the pros and cons." She presses her hands on the armrests. "Then I visualized my daughter running around that camp, in a red bathing suit."

"You knew that camp?"

"No. But my daughter looked perfectly at ease there."

"You felt at ease too?"

She nods. "I was about to leave the room, to buy a red bathing suit for her." She inhales deeply. "And the phone rang."

"Was it your daughter?"

"Yes." She bites her lip. "She wanted a red bathing suit!"

How do we handle friction at home?

"I attended a conflict management seminar at work," says Jerome, Marketing Director of a cosmetic company. "Then, I applied the techniques on my wife."

"They worked?"

"No." His lips flutter. "They failed, miserably."

"Give me an example."

"The other day, we had a fight about buying a refrigerator." He sniffs. "I had already worked out her personality-type, and placed her on my conflict management matrix."

"You've been anticipating the conflict."

He nods. "But, as soon as I started applying those techniques, she left the room silently, and started the laundry."

"She ignored you altogether."

"She said I bored her to death." He shrugs. "I don't think friction with colleagues has the same chemistry as the friction with spouse."

"What's different?"

"In a stable home, friction is inherent."

"Sounds contradictory."

"Okay, let me explain." He presses the arms of his chair. "Similarity makes friends, right?" He stands. "But, what makes a durable couple?"

"Complementarity."

"Complementarity is the opposite of similarity." He turns toward me. "Naturally, in a durable relation, the partners rarely think alike. That causes a lot of frictions."

"How do you avoid those?"

"I don't." He sits on the edge of the table. "Those frictions generate alternatives."

"What kind?"

"Constructive." He rubs his hands. "Ones that neither of us could have thought otherwise."

"Why do people separate then, saying they're too different from each other?"

"They take the easy way out of conflicts." He taps the table. "But, they're wrong."

"Wouldn't they have been better off with someone similar?"

"Then we're confusing friendship with love." He walks to the end of the room. "What happens when you bring two positive ions together?"

"They repulse each other."

"A husband and wife, with qualities too similar, do exactly the same."

"Why?"

"Isn't it irritating to be around someone who imitates you all the time?"

"I agree."

"On the contrary, when your wife has a set of expertise very different from yours, you just leave her alone."

"And, when her set of expertise is too close to yours, you keep nagging her about doing everything *exactly* the same way you would do."

"That's the point!" He raises his thumb. "Then, out of that obsession, frustration surfaces in that household. And that plants the seed of incompatibility in that couple."

"On the other hand, if you two complement each other, you remain compatible."

"That's the virtue of complementarity." He takes a pen out of his pocket. "I let my wife lead me in the areas she's an expert. And she does the same with me. There is no duplication, no waste of energy."

"Complementarities should never break a household then?"

"No, as long as we keep friction within bounds." The pen clinks in his hand. "But, if friction generates too much heat, we can burn up what we created by complementarities."

"How do *you* keep friction within limits?"

"I respect my wife." The pen traces the word 'RESPECT'. "And I can do that because I respect myself, for who I am and what I do." He puts the pen back in his pocket. "There is one area, however, where similarity is important for a couple."

I turn my chair toward him.

"The basic values." He walks to his seat. "We have complementary qualities, but we have similar values at our core." He sits down. "Since we *never* do anything that contradicts our common values, our friction never goes out of hands."

"When you chose each other, how did you make sure you had similar values?"

"We didn't let others tell us that." His index sways. "We didn't beat our values to death over dinners either."

He rolls his sleeve. "We chose each other because it felt natural to be together." He taps the desk. "We stayed together because we felt no resistance from inside."

Two more issues generate dangerous friction within our conjugal lives.

The first is: *when we judge our internal passion by external benchmarks*.

"I bought my partner a life insurance on his birthday," says Muriel, a 29 years-old nurse. "Most won't find this romantic, but—"

"You do."

"One has to think of the children on the way."

"Then the life insurance becomes the most romantic gift."

"A couple may start out with a boiling passion." She brushes aside the bangs from her forehead. "But, that passion either evaporates, or…"

"Condenses, to give life."

"That's it!" A dimple dents her cheek. "Condenses into spirituality, to raise a family. Sounds natural, isn't it?" She frowns. "But, others think I'm nuts."

"Does it really mater?"

"No." She purses her lips. "What really matters is how our relation has evolved."

"How?"

"When the weeds of our passion cleared, we saw the roots that bind us together."

The second is: *when we seek external opinions to resolve our internal issues.*

During a bicycle trip, I meet an eighty-three year old stork breeder. He has twenty-eight couples of these birds in his garden, and one in separation. In the legends, storks always stay together for life, but this couple, after having raised chicks for twelve consecutive years, has separated.

"Did they learn from us?" The old man sighs. "Look at their beautiful nest. That's where they raised all their babies."

The nest parks on a three-foot column. The male perches on the nest, while the female pecks around, never farther than ten yards from the base of the column.

I crouch. "Do they hurt each other?"

"No."

"Does the male occupy the nest all the time?"

"No. He leaves her the nest some days."

"They just don't occupy the nest together anymore. That's all?"

Another stork hovers over the nest, and then sits on an apple tree. The male stands up. His wings spread, his tail rises, his throat inflates, his neck bends backward, and his beaks clack. The female mirrors his movements.

The intruder flies off.

The man scratches his head, glances at me. "That baffles me somewhat."

I stand up. "Since they separated, did they take other partners?"

"No. Neither of them."

"Who told you they separated?"

"Here." The man raises a book. "And they dispute too."

The female walks two steps toward us, and then freezes.

The man touches my shoulder. "She has seen a worm's head coming out of the ground."

I sit down again and follow her immobile gaze.

The male jumps off and lands on the grass; the female's pupil dilates immediately.

A sharp wind dislodges a branch from the nest. The female rushes to it, and tucks the branch back in its place.

The man scratches his chin. "I better put this book away in the shade."

"For how long are you breeding storks?"

"Thirty-six years."

"When did you buy that book?"

"Two years ago."

"Why?"

"I couldn't resolve their disputes."

In dispute, watch your partner's acts; they speak more than the words.

How do we renew the collective self of our family?

Some do through adventures.

During another bicycle expedition, an extraordinary family grabs my attention: a bearish father, an athletic mother, and their three kids—all traveling on bicycles, with bags bulging on both sides of their carriers. Even the youngest kid, no more than six or seven, carries two bags on his bike, one at the front and one at the back.

The woman in lead squints at a map through a magnifying glass. Because I know this route well, I approach them to help.

"How did we find this route?" She pushes the sunglasses over her head. "I called the tourist office, asked for the most popular destinations, and then chose the farthest from those."

"You bet." Her husband wipes sweat off his forehead. "Marie has gone crazy."

Marie fixes her husband with a stare. "Our children love this experience, but Pierre is still coming out of his fear."

"Fear!" Pierre shrieks. "Other than you, Monsieur, we haven't seen a single soul for the last thirty kilometers. We don't even know if we're going in the right direction."

"We're in vacation, Pierre. Why worry about directions?" Marie descends from her bike. "We have our camping supplies with us. We lose our path, and we pitch the tents in the forest." She tilts her head toward the blue-green foliage of pine, beyond the fields.

"Yes! Yes! Yes!" The children throw up their hands.

Pierre grimaces. "Are you nuts? Wild boars will puncture our bellies at night."

Marie's gaze lowers on her husband's paunch; his eyebrows rise and fall.

I wink at the children. "I saw one last night."

"Where? Where?" The children jump off their bikes.

"Far behind. He was on his way back from dinner, so he ignored me." I turn toward Marie. "How many kilometers you do per day?"

"Thirty…forty. All depends on Mathew." Marie touches her youngest child's head. "I'm amazed what our kids can do." She turns toward her husband. "Pierre, would you have known this ever?"

"I didn't know I could do forty a day. For sure, that's reassuring." Sweat drips off his forearm. "And refreshing."

Let's move to our external world now.

{Within our external world}

How do we renew our external world?

Through a change of perspective.

"When I lack ideas, I don't turn in place," says Benjamin, a 63 years-old painter, in his workshop. "I leave the city, and go to the void."

"Void?"

"Desert, ocean, mountains, or wherever you can see the horizon."

"You paint city life. Won't you find more details walking around a city?"

"That's what people don't understand about artists." He squares his shoulders. "Will you pay a thousand Euros for details you can see, by yourself, walking around this city?"

"What marks you the most outside city?"

"Maybe an owl." His brush points to a pair of eyes, goggling inside a dark tree over a house. "If I didn't leave once in a while, I'll be painting only people and their poodles."

"You leave to refresh your vision."

He turns back to his portrait. "I leave to remind me that the same life is flowing in all other creatures."

"How does the void help you see this?"

"In void, the universe looms over us. We see how tiny we are." He slides the curtain and points to the sky. "Here, we never look up. So, our ego blows out of proportions."

"After you return, your ego still remains within bounds?"

"For me, yes." He leans on an inclined desk. "The follies of others no longer tap on my nerves. No matter what they do, I know they're as small as I am."

"So you accept them the way they are."

He pushes away from the desk. "I even see their virtues."

"That's a big change of perspective!"

"In void, another magic happens." He strides to a portfolio of paintings.

I move with him.

He flaps through the sketches. "I close my eyes, and visualize the space between me and the Sun." His hand stops. "All of a sudden, impulses from the space reach into me."

"What do they do to you?"

"A lot." He closes the portfolio. "Sometimes, they even shake me." He sits on a stool. "Then, they pass. And I discover the truth."

"Which truth?"

"The right details have always been sitting inside me."

How do we avoid frictions with our external world?
Imagine a cluster of ports along the coast of an ocean.

Each port encloses a tiny part of that ocean inside. A breakwater protects that port from the large waves of the ocean, so the activities of the harbor can flourish.

The breakwater, however, doesn't disconnect the port from the ocean.

Whatever currents occur in the ocean also extends into the port; its water rises and falls in synchrony with the ocean, but only to a lesser degree. Each port moves in synchrony with the ocean, thus in synchrony with all other ports in the cluster; the ocean binds them all.

The Universal Self binds our Individual Selves.

Whatever currents occur in our external world also extend into us, but only to a lesser degree. We always move in synchrony with others around us, whether we want it or not; the *ether* of our collective self binds us all.

"You can cover yourself from head to toe. Then, cross your arms, clench your jaws, pinch your nose, clog your ears, and close your eyes." Louise, 28 years old, film crew, rubs her forehead. "Your flesh still gets the creeps, in a metro full of grumps."

"Why?"

"Because you want to avoid them." Her eyes avert. "That's what I did before, and it cost me a lot."

"What did it cost you?"

"Nobody would sit next to me."

"Why?"

She bites her lower lip. "People saw what I was doing. So, they ostracized me."

"Did that hurt you?"

"Not initially." She wipes her mouth. "But then I saw the truth: when I avoided others, I didn't trust myself either."

"That must have been scary."

She nods. "Then work took me to Mumbai."

Her eyes twinkle. "From the suburbs, I took a train to the city center everyday. You stand on the platform and,"—she sways her hands—"when the train comes, people just push you in."

"You learnt to go with the flow."

"And when you reach your destination, people again push you out." She sways her hands the other way.

"You saved energy for your film shoot."

"Then I saw I wasn't allergic anymore."

"Allergic?"

"Before, if someone's flesh touched mine, I would scream like a maniac. In Mumbai, I slipped in and out through those sweaty fleshes, without any problem."

"Why?"

"I don't know." She turns toward me. "But, that experience changed something inside me. Now I can smile again, even to the weirdest in my city."

"Do they smile back?"

"Yes!" She cocks her head. "First time this happened, I almost flipped over."

Her eyes bulge. "Then I said, 'Bonjour', and the person even replied. How do you think that happened?"

"People simply react to what they see on your face."

"Before, I let others do the smiling first. Now, I'm the first to smile."

"That does you good?"

"Yes." Her face twitches. "I no longer feel oppressed."

"What oppressed you?"

"I suffered from a horrible solitude before." Her fists clench. "I had a lot to say, and I wanted to share those with people next to me."

Her lips quiver. "But, because I didn't trust them, I couldn't share anything. Every time I came close to opening my mouth, my body would revolt."

"Then you changed your attitude."

"No. I resented others for not being accessible." Her head swerves. "I walked around like a balloon of anger, ready to explode, at the slightest friction."

I lean on my backrest.

"Everyone needs someone to talk to, Monsieur Garai, but…" She shakes her head. "We've made plain talk just impossible. So, what do we do? Throw ourselves on foods, or other stupid—"

"Louise, how did *you* change your attitude?"

"I lowered my pride."

"Being out of the context helped?"

"I think." She places her hands on the armrest. "I accepted that everything exists for a reason."

"Give me an example."

"Those I called 'losers' before, exist for a reason: to teach me a lesson."

"What lesson?"

"Change yourself first, before you try to change anyone."

How do we embrace our external world?
We've seen plenty of examples so far. Let's do some practice now.

Sit up straight. Then, close your eyes, relax your arms on your knees, and bring the tips of your index and thumb together; feel your digital pulses. Note the rhythm of their variations.

Let your mind run. Feel the movements of your lungs and heart. Visualize an empty space around you.

You'll notice: your digital pulses beat with your heart, and their sways move with your lungs.

When your mind has emptied out, you'll feel waves coming from your surrounding. And the waves of your pulses will move with them. When that happens, you've physically embraced your external world.

Practice this exercise in progressively broader contexts: at home, at work, in the metro, in a garden, on the seashore, on a mountain, in a different city, then a different country…

Your digital pulses will synchronize with all, progressively.

You'll discover the similarities in all; your prejudices against others will vanish; your regrets, resentments, and sorrow will disappear. As each day goes by, you'll embrace a world progressively bigger, in accordance with your self.

Your loneliness will leave you for ever.

When you progress with this exercise, you'll also experience the following: a vivid smell from the past, or a clear voice from your ancestors. You'll read thoughts of others, starting with your family, friends, and colleagues, and then going on to people in your external world. You'll progressively embrace all, across space and time.

Your fear of death will disappear.

All gains come with a price. Your enhanced sensibility opens you to the riches inside others, *and* to their ravages. But, if you've grown robust through wholesome living, you can secure the benefits, while resisting the damages.

There is one more issue to consider: action always produces reaction.

If the pulses from your surrounding resonate stronger within you, then the pulses from inside you will also resonate stronger in your surrounding. Your thoughts and actions will have stronger impacts upon others.

This requires you to have a robust sense of civic responsibilities.

Your wholesome living will give you that sense.

14: In conclusion

What comes next?

In my poll, 89% of the clients worried about this; the remaining 11% took life as it came.

I probed deeper into the self-confidence of those 11%. The vision of Katherine, 51 years old, manager of a railway station, marked me the most.

"It's not death that frightens us really," she says. "We all know we'll reach that end someday, but what scares the hell out of us is: *how* we would reach there."

"What are the main threats along the way?"

"Disability, disease, and destitution." She takes her glasses off. "Since Man learnt to read and write, that's where his efforts went."

"To develop a philosophy of life?"

"No. To prevent those sufferings on the way to the end."

"How do *you* prevent?"

"I don't want to live a hundred years, leaning on others." She pulls a tissue out of her bag. "I want to live, however long I'm meant to live, in dignity."

"What does it translate to, in your everyday life?"

"Do what feels right for me. And, do it whole-hearted." She wipes her glasses. "By doing that, I know I'll return to my origin gracefully."

"You think we return to the same place we came from?"

"I don't know." She puts her glasses on. "But, what really matters to me is: how I bridge the gap between my birth and death. What I do with my life, in between those two points, without having to worry about what comes next."

Consciously or unconsciously, we all accept we'll return to wherever we came from.

Nevertheless, most of us want to do this return as smoothly and as painlessly as possible. But, how?

By doing our task right.

The evolution of Man, between birth and death, is a round-trip process.

At birth, a part of the Universal Self enters our body, as Individual Self, to accomplish a unique task. We're not left alone, however. The Universe lays out a path for us; but, along that path, by our proactive efforts, we accomplish that task, and rejoin our origin.

This return occurs gracefully, when we remain aware of our evolution, during all our actions. The Universe has provided means for this awareness. Through our experiments, from the first day of life, we start discovering our Individual Self, as well as its relation with the rest.

Learning without challenges does not produce durable knowledge. In adolescence, when we enter into discordance with self, we encounter these challenges. Toward the end of this phase, when we seek a role in life, our convergence with the origin begins.

One of the two outcomes follows this stage.

If we execute our tasks right, in accordance with self, the process of union with our Individual Self deepens. If we don't, we separate from our self, and the process of degeneration begins.

When we have united with our Individual Self smoothly, all our anger, fear, temptations, and sorrow disappear. Our senses sharpen; we see our coherence with the world around, the Universal Self. Our journey toward origin proceeds with grace.

We are, by no means, left alone. The Universe provides guide, all along our way.

"I felt *particularly* alone, after my parents died," says Peggy, banker, married happily for seventeen years, with two kids, and a bubbling social life.

"Why particularly?"

"My parents have always been present in my life." She rubs her palm. "In my adolescence, like everyone else, I rebelled." She straightens her back. "But, when something serious came up, I always ran to them."

"Did you do the same as adult?"

"Not exactly." She scratches the tip of her nose. "I don't think we can really stop depending on supportive parents. At least, I couldn't."

"Even after you had your own children?"

"Yes." She rolls her shoulders back. "Sounds strange, but it's true. Unconsciously, I kept looking up to them, for experience. How do the orphans do?"

"They learn to look inside themselves, earlier than others."

"Really?" She frowns, then looks afar.

"Anyway, once I lost my job." Her eyes moisten. "Normally, I would have run to my father, but he had passed away the year before."

I lean forward.

She rubs her chin. "So I started visualizing him. Thought, real hard, what he would have told me." Her eyes shut and her lips tremble.

I lean back.

She startles. "And something moved inside me." She opens her eyes, and rubs her forearm.

"The answer you were looking for, came from within you?"

"I felt my father here." She presses her chest. "I saw his hand extend toward me from the Universe."

"Did you notice something different about you afterward?"

"Yes." A smile spreads across her face. "I abandoned all fears after that."

"Why?"

"Because I know he is in me, always." She puts her purse on the floor. "All this could have been very dangerous for me, Monsieur Garai."

"Dangerous?"

"Faith can save us from peril." Her eyes glare. "But, faith can also push us toward peril."

"How?"

"You know the *merchants* of faith today." She covers her throat. "I almost succumbed to one."

"Who pulled you out?"

"Dad." She exhales. "He caught me by the shoulders, stared right into my eyes, and said: 'Peggy, do what feels right for you. And do it sincerely. That's the only thing that will save you in this world.'"

What ensures our smooth return to the origin?
Doing our task right, in accordance with self.

Every one of us comes with a specific task, as part of a bigger plan. None is thrown upon this world, just to thrash around, and then taken back. Everyone's task is unique, and equally important. As long as we discover that task, and carry it out with our best efforts, we return smoothly toward our origin.

On the way back, if we keep the eyes of our mind open, we feel our evolution; we see the panorama of our internal landscape. *These are the only durable compensations, for doing our task right.* Everything else, material or not, serves only as means to this journey. The key to our lasting well-being is: seeing this evolution, while doing our task right.

Only 3% of the people in my poll could state with clarity how they, and not just their skills, evolved from one point to another, as a result of doing their tasks. What did they do differently from the rest?

In their diaries, they recorded the snapshots of their evolution regularly.

When we work with awareness of this evolution, we see the ray of life ahead. The thought of growing senile never occurs to us. With our inner self enriched, we forge ahead leaner—materially, physically, and psychologically.

We become spiritually lean.

Can we still enjoy life?
The lean enjoys life much more than the engorged.

Leanness sharpens our senses; less yields more for us.

During a hike in the high mountains, I sprain my ankle. At this altitude, weather changes with the blink of an eye. I take out my mobile phone, but hesitate to call for help.

"Son of a bitch!" A female voice grumbles from behind a rock.

I spring up, alarmed.

She huffs up the trail. "My mood is so horrible today."

A man, with only one arm, follows her, nonchalantly. They drop their rucksacks near me, and exhale together.

I scan the man's stump. In so many places, this steep trail narrows to a foot or two, and ragged gorges line its sides.

He looks at my bare foot. "Are you alright?"

"Yes." I've forgotten my pain.

His gaze wanders into the clouds gliding below us, over the intersection of two glaciers.

"Hungry?" The woman hands me a sandwich.

"Thanks." I take it. "Is this your first—"

"Hell, no!" She grumbles again. "He has done the chains of Peru, Chili, and Patagonia. Even the Himalayas." Her jaws clench. "What a pain in—"

"I never asked you to come with me." The man grins.

She rolls her eyes, and blows a large puff of air.

"I'll tell you something, Mister." He drops his ice-axe and touches my shoulder. "She never regrets her raptures at these heights."

Her eyes narrow. She places her hands on the hips.

I scrutinize their faces. "What marks you the most at these heights?"

He takes a sip from his bottle, then wipes his face. "How your body can get by with so little."

"What do you mean?"

"Your lungs with so little oxygen, your stomach with so little food." He picks up the ice-axe, and wipes its handle on his parka. "And, your brain with so little certitude."

"Are you a professional guide?"

"I'm a laborer at a supermarket." He crushes a rock with the adze of his axe. "It helps to get away from all that, once in a while."

"But, why push yourself to such extremes?"

"You ever go to supermarkets, Mister?"

"Yes."

"What do you see?"

"Excess."

"If you spent your days surrounded by that, wouldn't you want to make sure your body still remembers how to get by with less?"

A drunk never appreciates wines.

But a true expert knows how to taste one, and then move on to the next. While sipping a little, he doesn't forget to sharpen his tongue, and feel its evolution. A true expert keeps his body, mind, and senses lean.

He remains spiritually lean.

With a lean spirit, not only our senses become sharper, but also the range of our enjoyment enlarges. We don't push aside pain, and cling to pleasure. Our lean spirit converts pain into pleasure, and assimilates all into our evolution. Nothing frightens us; nothing obsesses us; nothing fails to contribute to our evolution.

We embrace all.

A lean spirit: does it really exist?
We've seen them all along in this book.

What do these people have that make them different from the rest?
Their confidence.

They have confidence in their Individual Self; they have confidence in the Universal Self that envelops them. They know their tasks. And they carry those out sincerely, with full awareness of their evolution, always in line with their fundamental belief.

A man with confidence never fears; a man with confidence never loses temper; a man with confidence never drowns in sorrow; a man with confidence never gives up.

A man with confidence always runs in balance.

Do we need role models for this?
No.

On this path, your only reference is: *you.*

We may make mistakes on our way. But, if we remain aware of our evolution, these mistakes bring out the best teacher from inside. We transform these stumbling blocks into our stepping stones, and forge ahead better equipped.

As long as we live wholesome, and do what feels right, nothing can ever destroy our spirit.

The confidence in our fundamental belief generates values within us—values that are uniquely personal. When we live by these values, internal conflicts never arise. When we carry out our task whole-heartedly, in line with these values and in awareness of our evolution, existential problems cease to exist in our world.

Unwell-being never raises its head within us.

15: Paving our way out

Auguste Rodin said: Sculpture is the art of holes and lumps.

You choose a block, chop off what you don't need, and you obtain what was inside your head. You don't invent anything new.

In reconstructing yourself from strain, you simply rediscover yourself. Each step opens your eyes to your inner self, and its relation with the rest. If you remain aware of your evolution along the way, these discoveries fuel your enthusiasm.

But, others may appreciate only your final form.

One day in Kolkata, in front of my hotel, I notice a tent.

Everyday, a man goes in at dusk, and comes out at dawn. A sheer curtain covers the tiny window on the side. Inside, skeletons of straw line the tarpaulin walls. A week later, coarse patches of clay cover those skeletons. The week after, garlands of ugly lumps circle their throats.

Few more weeks pass. One dawn, the artist taps on my shoulder from behind.

"Kali, the goddess of time. You want to buy one?"

"I would have, if I had a place to store." I move back from the window. "But I really appreciate your diligence inside this solitary tent."

He invites me inside.

I scan the beautiful statues. "Why do you keep your tent closed always?"

"You peep through everyday. Did they inspire you before?"

No, they gave me nightmares. "How could you spend your days and nights—?"

"With them, when they looked so ugly and horrible, huh?" He laughs. "Do you know what you looked like, for nine months, in your mother's womb?"

"I do. Thanks."

He cracks open a bottle of paint. "My mind saw, long ago, what your eyes are seeing now."

"It's good you don't show others the intermediate stages."

"Of course." He frowns. "Other than me, why should anyone else see them?"

"Unless they're close to you. Or, they're your apprentices."

He picks up a brush. "Even with them, I keep my sacred garden secret at times."

"Why?"

He dips the brush in paint. "I'll dilute my work otherwise."

"To them?"

"No." He paints the tongue of the statue in scarlet. "The creation will lose its charm to *me*, and the end product will be something banal."

"I see. So, your vision of the final beauty pulls you through the ugly stages?"

He stops. "Beauty feeds upon the ugly."

"Sorry?"

"Have you ever worked in a garden?"

"Yes."

"Flowers grow upon compost, right?"

"Absolutely."

"Now, let me ask you this." He drops the brush. "Who told you those intermediate stages are ugly for me?"

While you reconstruct yourself, maintain your privacy. Otherwise, what you reconstruct will not resemble you at the end.

Hold that dignified end image of yourself firmly in your mind; you'll plough through the intermediate stages, ugly or beautiful, with the joy of reality.

Rodin says: inside you there is that artist, whose existence you ignore.

That artist does not only want to see how you look under the cool moon. That artist also wants to see how you look under the blazing sun, the tempestuous wind, the torrential rain, and the hideous fog.

Can you do this reconstruction, embracing all?

Yes. You've done it before; you can only do it better now.

Save your notes. Later, when you look at them, they'll still reveal something new about you.

Patrick from chapter 11 saved his notes. They saved him later, by helping him recover his fundamental belief, and by aligning accordance with his self.

An Afro-American from Connecticut, Patrick grew up in a family of five children. His father worked at a local church; his mother, at an elementary school. With modest means but abundant dignity, both parents educated their children in the simple rules of good living, and then let them live freely.

Patrick often accompanied his father to the services of their church.

His father would say to the local teenagers sunken in despair: 'There is a force that binds us all. Do your part, whole-hearted, and you won't fall apart.'

"Dad, why do you say that to these kids?" Patrick says one evening, on their way back home. "What if they don't want to believe in God?"

"Who is asking them to believe in God? All I'm saying is: believing in you alone is not enough. You feel isolated."

Patrick isn't convinced. "Nobody stands behind these kids. So, why give them that illusion?"

"Pat, are you asking if there is really a binding force?"

"Why should I have that faith?" Patrick shoves his hands in the pockets.

"Certainly not because I tell you." Dad taps Patrick's chest. "Let's see: who keeps running everything inside you?"

"My brain."

"When you die, it's still there. Why everything stops then?"

"Come on, Dad! That's an over-killed cliché." Patrick blows. "Life leaves my body when I die."

266

Dad stops. "What's life?"

Patrick scratches his head. "A force."

"Now, let's look outside you. What makes fresh leaves grow on that tree?"

"Life." The same force.

"What makes a glacier melt into river?"

"Heat." Another force.

"What makes water evaporate into cloud?"

"The same force."

"Who brings rain down to earth?"

"Gravity." Still another force.

"Who keeps the moon orbiting around us?"

The same force. "Okay, okay. Force, in one form or another, holds things together. But, there are explosions too."

"That's the same force, in destructive form." Dad strides forward. "That's exactly what I try to prevent for these kids."

"Sorry, Dad." Patrick catches up with him. "I don't understand you."

"Pat." Dad turns his head. "These kids have a force inside them. You can see that in their will to change." He touches Patrick's forearm. "They want to get out of their misery, change their lives for better."

"Why don't they?"

"They would, if they didn't feel so isolated."

Patrick kicks a stone. "You lost me!"

"Look." Dad grabs Patrick's elbow. "When these kids don't see that binding force in their life, they feel alone."

Does Patrick feel like this? Yes. He wants to discuss so many things with Dad, but...

Dad pulls him by the arm. "They do stupid things, and they perish."

"But, Dad!" Patrick halts. "Shouldn't that force bind them?"

"Yes." Dad releases Patrick's arm. "Only if they do their part right."

"You're confusing me again."

"There is no free ride, Pat." Dad turns to look at him. "Each has to do his part, sincerely. If you don't, you're replaced."

Scary. Patrick bites his nail.

"But, it's a force of cohesion, not oppression." Dad opens his arms. "You only gain by putting in your efforts. Everyone gains at the end."

Patrick chips his lips. "How do I know where to put my efforts?"

"In a cause *you* consider worthy." Dad strikes Patrick's chest with his knuckles. "Once you decide on that cause, devote your whole heart to it. And leave the rest to that binding force."

"Dad!" Patrick clutches his chest. "You punched me on the heart; it hurts like hell."

"I wanted to carve those words on your heart."

"You very well did." Patrick tries to catch up his breath. "How do I know what's worthy for me?"

"Listen to your heart."

His heart still thuds. "What if I don't?"

"Life will show you then." Dad rubs Patrick's chest. "And, you'll have a chance to correct your mistake."

Everyone Patrick knows has had a chance, but not everyone came out right. Can he still fix his errors with Tessa?

"If I believe in that binding force, what happens?"

"Your will stays alive, and you change."

That's what Patrick tries. But, nothing ever goes the way he wants.

"Pat, you're rubbing your sole on the ground. Let me show you something." Dad pulls him by the shoulder. "See that star up there?"

Patrick traces Dad's index. So many of them! A canopy of twinkles.

Dad twirls Patrick by the shoulder. "What do they look like to you now?"

"A spangle." Patrick's ears buzz. "On the dress of a black girl, exquisitely beautiful."

"That's Tessa in your head." Dad clears his throat. "Now, leave Tessa with me here, and go up there, near that star."

Patrick closes his eyes, flies to that star.

"Now, look down." Dad's voice falls a few notches. "What does our town look like from there?"

"A cluster of glowworms."

"And, Tessa?"

"A tiny worm in that cluster."

"And, her love for you?"

"A fleeting impulse in that worm."

"Now, open your eyes, and listen carefully." Dad turns Patrick again, and then faces him. "That star up there existed *long* before you and I were born."

Patrick's brain fizzes. "Then, what do we see up there?"

"Its phantom."

"What!"

"The light that's reaching us right now could be three thousand years old."

Patrick gasps. "Really?"

"And, the last light emitted from that star could take three thousand more years to reach our earth." Dad's eyes twinkle. "Now, try to see Tessa, a millennium ahead. What does she look like?"

A phantom. Goose bumps tingle all over Patrick.

"Swarms our head, right?" Dad wraps his arm around Patrick. "You and I, and all our problems here, could be nothing but phantoms in someone's head up there, in that galaxy, thousands of light years away."

His teeth glitter in moonlight. "Six thousand years old phantoms, Pat. Who knows?"

"Dad!" Patrick quakes. "It's chilly out here, let's go home."

When we want to change, it's our willpower which counts the most, not our age.

270

One night, walking down the seafront of Mumbai, I trip over something.

"Do you want to measure your weight?" A rumpled face grins on a neck of rope. "One rupee only." He points to a scale on the footpath.

"No thanks."

Annoyed, I move on, but his grin lingers inside me.

Around three in the morning, unable to fall asleep, I leave my hotel, walk back to the same spot on the waterfront, and tap on his shoulder. His white head emerges from under a crumpled shawl.

"Do you want to check your weight now?"

"Yes." I hold out a ten-rupee note.

He squints. "It's one rupee only."

"Well, give me the change then." I pick up the scale and check its accuracy.

"It's high quality." He grins. "Made in Germany."

"Where did you buy it?"

"I didn't buy it. One day, an obese woman rolled out of her car, and dumped it over there." He points to the curb.

I sit next to him. "Tell me, where do you come from?"

"From a small village in Bihar." He sits up.

"What brought you here?"

"The floods. I lost my son, his wife, and their three kids—all in one morning." He folds his knees to the chest. "I had nothing left back there, so I came here to start a new life."

"How old are you?"

He rests his chin between the kneecaps, and wraps his arms around the legs. "Seventy, plus a few years."

"How did you start here?"

"I didn't beg." His back straightens; his chin comes off his knees. "I slept here, and survived on the leftovers from those shops." He points toward the snack-stalls lining the beach. "Then, one day my luck landed on the street." He lifts the scale to his forehead.

"Do you really believe this scale would change your life?"

"It already has." He jingles a pouch. "I need fifty more clients to stand on this scale, and I'll have the money I need."

"What will you do with that money?"

"I'll buy a train ticket." He slides the pouch under his jute rug. "Then, I'll go back to my village."

"Why do you want to go back there now?"

"I've overcome my grief." His eyes lower. "Now, I've work to do there."

"Will you start from zero again?"

His eyes beam. "Yes." A smile lifts his cheek, and creases the skin around his eyes.

Warmth flows through me. "Can I buy you a train ticket?"

He touches my shoulder. "No, my son." He hands me the note back. "Take your money. You didn't stand on my scale."

If we live in accordance with our self, neither age nor hardship ever shrivels our dignity.

And, we never feel alone.

272

As Rodin says, unknown forces exist in this Nature.

When we do our part right, she lends those forces to us. She shows what our eyes never see; she reveals what our mind never understands. We may not see the results of our actions right away, but these forces *always* collaborate with our sincere efforts.

One summer, at an orphanage in Kolkata, a toddler grips my calf.

"He needs more affection than others." A Sister takes him away from me.

"Why?" I follow them.

"When he was two years old, he was dumped in a garbage bin."

I stop.

The toddler sobs. The Sister leads him down the corridor, and his eyes implore me till the bend.

'Adopt! Adopt!' My heart thumps.

'Impractical.' My brain knocks back.

Outside the orphanage, my brain triumphs over my heart.

But, at the lunch table, my guts knot. I leave the food, walk into the lawn of Victoria Memorial, and sink on a bench. Couples loaf around, hand-in-hand, in this languid afternoon.

"What makes species leap?" I mumble.

"Mutation." Darwin rumbles.

"What makes a man leap?"

"Courage."

"What will happen to this toddler?"

"Only the fittest survive." His eyelids flap. "What can you do?"

Nothing. My guts release; sleep drifts me away.

A church bell tolls four. I spring up, drenched in sweat; the toddler's face disperses in the blazing sun. My grandmother's voice echoes in my head: "Cower if you dare, in front of responsibility, but never deny the power of your wish."

I make a long wish for the toddler, and leave the park.

Three weeks later, I arrive at the airport, to catch an overnight flight to Europe. Behind me, four European couples join the queue; in their white arms, brown babies garble with joy.

My heart aches again for the toddler.

Inside the plane, two rows ahead of me, an Italian couple lays a dark baby, wrapped in a white jumpsuit. After hesitating for a while, I walk over to their row and greet them.

The woman tucks the baby's feet under a blanket, and pulls the hood of the jumpsuit over the head.

"How long did you wait to get all the papers?" I ask.

"Ten months." The man exhales.

"Did you have to stay here all this time?"

"No."

"We both work, so we had to come back several times." The woman wipes saliva off the baby's cheek. "In fact, this was our fourth trip."

"You made four trips in ten months!"

"We weren't sure this time either." The man shakes his head. "All happened at the last hour."

"Good luck." I return to my seat.

I calculate the number of days away from work, and the money spent. The stewardess dims the lights.

At dawn, a baby's cry grips my guts. I spring from my seat and dart to the row of the Italian couple.

"Sorry for the noise." The woman lulls the baby in her arms. "He's having a nightmare."

I gasp. "Can you take his hood off?"

Confused, she does; a chill sweeps through me.

I touch the man's shoulder. "When did you get the papers for him?"

"Beginning of this week." He squints.

I cover my mouth.

"Why?" The woman frowns. "Is there something wrong with this kid?"

"No! No!" I step back. "Everything is fine."

I try to smile at the toddler; he returns me an intent look.

The man grips my wrist. "Do you know this baby?"

"No." I hold my breath. "Absolutely not."

"Oh, you scared us." He lets my wrist go. "What happened this time was a miracle."

I return to my seat and wipe my tears. The passenger next to me opens the shutter. The saffron sun rushes in and warms my face.

For most, well-being doesn't come on a silver platter.

Among my clients, 68% spin their wheels of childhood misery into late adulthood, for an average of five years, even after they've succeeded in life. Then one day, by sheer willpower, they change strategy: they channel their energy into discovering what pulled them out of misery, not what plunged them into it.

And they recover their fundamental belief!

From that exit point, when they look back at their lives, they see it's the same belief that has driven them all along. And, in most situations, they've stayed in accordance with their self.

Their regrets and resentments vanish at once; they become spiritually lean.

A lean organism streamlines energy. The thoughts that come in accordance with our self have more chance of magnifying into actions. Allow me to explain this through an analogy.

We know a lever magnifies effort. Two factors determine this magnification:

- the ratio of leverage between the two arms of the lever;
- and the level of friction at its fulcrum of balance.

A large ratio and a low friction produce a high magnification.

In the same manner, two factors determine the magnification of our thoughts into actions:

-the leverage between our intimate conviction and willpower;
-and the friction at the fulcrum of our dynamic balance.

When internal resistance is absent, a solid intimate conviction, leveraged by a strong willpower, produces a gigantic magnification of thoughts into actions.

When does this happen?
When we act in accordance with our self.

Absence of internal resistance, a solid intimate conviction, and a strong willpower—all flow naturally out of this accordance.

We never fall out of our equilibrium. Emergencies may jolt us occasionally, but we regain our balance quickly.

Do these emergencies serve anything?
Yes.

They send sparks to the darkest corners of us. They wake up our hormones and neurotransmitters. They remove the rust from our body and mind. They show us we can still handle crises with poise.

Emergencies push us to our limits.

At those limits, the best inside us comes out. The eyes of our mind open, exceptional visions occur to us, and we have a chance to become extraordinary.

Does everyone become extraordinary at those limits?
No.

At those limits, extraordinary revelations do occur to everyone, but not everyone can translate those visions into proportional actions, and become extraordinary. Only those with solid intimate conviction, strong willpower, and no internal conflicts can do this.

That's where accordance with self becomes an absolute necessity.

Extraordinary revelations also come with their risks. What protects us at those limits?

Our civic sense and resistance to illusions.

Wholesome living, in accordance with self, renders us robust. A sharp civic sense breeds inside us, and we resist all illusions. We go to our limits, meet those revelations with our best tools from within, and become what we're meant to be.

Wholesome living, in accordance with self, is the path to our best.

Epilogue

Intuitively, we all know the rules of good living.

But, when stress invades us, we set these rules aside, and slide down the path led by stress. At that point, a subtle and poised guidance is often all we need, to trust our instincts again, and to put our intuitions back to work.

Subsequently, realigning accordance with our self, respecting our core values, and living wholesome—all flow from within us, naturally.

Long before I became a therapist, this universal truth had marked me.

When I worked in business, I saw how my colleagues and friends often ignored this, and suffered terribly. I started collecting data and analyzing them in my courses on stress management. This gave me a hypothesis on how degeneration begins for us, when we lose accordance with our self.

But, only after I delved deeper with the clients in my stress management practice, I could confirm that hypothesis:

Accordance with self is the key to our durable well-being.

You too knew this intuitively—didn't you?—before you started reading this book.

A prayer adapted from Veda

From confusions among illusions, guide me into the focus of reality;

From obscurity of inertia, guide me into the rays of proactivity;

From death in misery, guide me toward the exit with dignity.

******